Dale Spender is a feminist. She is a researcher and author who has written/edited more than thirty books on women's education, language and ideas. Among her publications are *Learning to Lose: Sexism and Education*, with Elizabeth Sarah (The Women's Press, 1980), *Feminist Theorists: Three Centuries of Women's Intellectual Traditions* (The Women's Press, 1983), *For The Record: The Making and Meaning of Feminist Knowledge* (The Women's Press, 1985), *Man Made Language* and *Women of Ideas – and What Men Have Done to Them*. She now lives in Brisbane, Australia, where she is working in the area of information technology, and women and brains.

Also by Dale Spender from The Women's Press:

Learning to Lose: Sexism and Education,
with Elizabeth Sarah (1980)
*Feminist Theorists: Three Centuries of
Women's Intellectual Traditions* (1983)
*For the Record: The Making and Meaning of
Feminist Knowledge* (1985)

DALE SPENDER

INVISIBLE WOMEN

WOMEN

The Schooling Scandal

Introduced by Sue Adler

Published by The Women's Press 1989
A member of the Namara Group
34 Great Sutton Street, London EC1V 0DX

Reprinted 1992

First published in Great Britain by Writers and Readers
Publishing Cooperative Society Ltd in association with
Chameleon Editorial Group 1982

British Library Cataloguing in Publication Data

Spender Dale
Invisible women: the schooling scandal.
1. Great Britain. Schools. Students: Girls.
Education. Equal of opportunity
1. Title
376′.941

ISBN 0-7043-4146-8

Printed in Great Britain by Cox and Wyman Ltd,
Reading, Berks.

Contents

Acknowledgements

I am deeply indebted to many women, particularly those in education, who have so freely shared their work with me and so readily discussed some of these issues. Without the help of Katherine Clarricoates and Michelle Stanworth, I would not have been able to document the magnitude of this problem and I am very grateful for their assistance and support. I also wish to thank Elizabeth Sarah who acts as a constant sounding board without ever showing signs of impatience or fatigue. My sister, Lynne Spender, who at some considerable cost has assumed at times the persona of a patriarchal critic, has also been invaluable in itemising 'the worst they can say'.

The librarians at the Fawcett Library deserve more than acknowledgement for the friendly and competent assistance they provide and for their forbearance when it comes to my overdue books. The women at the Women's Research and Resources Centre have been not only helpful but enthusiastic and I am grateful for their warmth and understanding. And I have a debt to Glynis Butcher, who typed the manuscript, which I cannot hope to repay.

Introduction to the 1989 edition

When *Invisible Women* was first published in 1981, feminist classroom teachers gave it a warm welcome. Here was acknowledgement of their own experience, of male control of mixed-sex classrooms; and plenty of useful, quotable data. It was a source of inspiration and of confirmation; a combination of women's history, analysis of contemporary educational practice and visions of a (better) future. Here too was the seed of Dale Spender's subsequent works – titles such as *Women of Ideas and what men have done to them, For the Record: the making and meaning of feminist knowledge, Feminist Theorists: three centuries of women's intellectual traditions*, all of them contributions to putting women 'on the record', so that future generations of feminists should not have to begin again to discover the history of women's political struggles. Republishing *Invisible Women*, too, is a contribution to the preservation of women's knowledge.

Since that first publication, there have been major changes in the British educational world, and an Education Act has been passed whose effects we cannot yet know. What we do know is that the old, old problem of sexism remains fundamentally untouched. Throughout a whole century of compulsory education in Britain, what and how we are taught has been decided by men – by white men of the dominant class – and determined by the needs of the male world. Dale Spender in this book brilliantly demonstrates how in our education system male subjectivity is given the appearance of objective fact. She describes sexism as 'no bias which can be eliminated, but the foundation stone of learning and education in our male-controlled society'.

Dale Spender's documentation of the exclusion of women from knowledge produced by men is also to be seen within a wider view of inequality. As she locates the problem in power and control, she notes in her introduction that 'Blacks, working-class people, old people, non-heterosexual people, disabled people could make exactly the same case as that made for women'. Analyses of the complex relationship between racism and sexism have been more fully developed by other writers since *Invisible Women* was written, especially by Black women writers, theorists and educationalists. Increasingly, educationalists and parents have demanded that educational policy also be seen in the light of power relations between white and black women; between white women teachers and Black girl students. I would hope that such an awareness of oppression and resistance should be the context for the reading (or re-reading) of this book in 1989.

Invisible Women assembles historical evidence of this male control of learning and relates it to current classroom and curricula, current policy and practice. And her 1981 analysis is no less applicable to the 1988 Education Reform Act and its related documents.

The 1988 Act makes the most fundamental changes in our education system of the century. It details alteration to the curriculum, administration and government of state schools, and demands the testing of all state school students at ages seven, eleven, fourteen and sixteen. And some of the rhetoric of liberalism and liberal feminism has actually been adopted by the policy makers. Gender has been on the agenda of the authors of the National Curriculum proposals for mathematics, science and English – the three core subjects identified in the Act. The related documents in each case include a brief section on equality of opportunity for girls and boys (alongside sections on ethnic and cultural diversity, and special needs). Girls, then, and black people, are just visible. But they are there as problems, on the periphery. The National Curriculum proposal on science, for instance, comments only on *girls'* attitudes and expectations; on girls' 'limitations'. Yet for years feminist educationists, as Dale Spender shows, have recognised the crucial importance of *teachers'* expectations, and the systematic devaluation of girls by male teachers, especially in maths and science.

The National Curriculum 5–16 consultation document states that 'All pupils, regardless of sex, ethnic origin and geographical location, have access to broadly the same good and relevant curriculum.' Is equal access possible in a sexist, racist society? Who determines what is 'good and relevant'? Good for whom? Relevant to whom? Throughout her book, Dale Spender challenges the authority of white men to decide what is appropriate and beneficial for all, and she challenges the assumption that their necessarily limited perspective is universal and bias-free. The GCSE criteria include a sentence proclaiming a 'bias-free' approach. But history is described in 1986 as 'Primarily concerned with recreating mankind's past'. Research undertaken by Heather Morris on GCSE English setbooks on the advisory lists of all six exam boards in 1988 reveals that, of 105 prose writers 81 are men; of 50 dramatists 49 are men.

In brief, the new legislation imposes central control, and a subject-defined curriculum essentially the same as that prescribed by the Board of Education as far back as 1904. Only the 'housewifery for girls/manual work for boys' divide of the earlier document is missing. The small step of a common curriculum on offer to girls and boys hardly compensates for the out-dated approach to learning. Current attempts to encourage girls and young women into scientific and technical vocations are linked to demands from industry, not egalitarian principles.

In addition to legislation under the Education Act, educationalists in the 1990s will be affected by the Local Government Act (1988). The notorious Section 28 of that Act prevents a local authority from:
(a) intentionally promoting homosexuality or publishing material with the intention of promoting homosexuality;
(b) promoting the teaching in any maintained school of the acceptability of homosexuality as a pretended family relationship.

To date, no legal challenges have been made in the courts, but the impact of Section 28 has been to promote bigotry to the homophobes and to promote self-censorship to the timid.

Men still dominate in senior positions in schools. In her chapter entitled 'Setting up the system' Dale Spender considers reasons for the disparity between women in senior positions, and in the teaching profession as a whole. An update of statistics shows that the trend continues, despite the Sex Discrimination Act (1975):

WOMEN TEACHERS	1965	1974	1986
Primary schools			
All	74%	77%	79%
Heads	51%	43%	46%
Deputy Heads	62%	60%	61%
Secondary schools			
All	41%	43%	46%
Heads	24%	19%	17%
Deputy Heads	40%	35%	30%
			(source: DES)

Outside state-controlled education, many of the centres of

women's education described in *Invisible Women* still exist, still characterised by what Virginia Woolf called 'the reprehensible poverty of our sex.' But the Feminist Library, previously Women's Research and Resources Centre, lost its funding in June 1988, making London the only capital city in Europe without a publicly funded women's library. That it continues is due to the commitment and energy of volunteers. It is currently housed at A Woman's Place; its future precarious. The Fawcett Library remains a wonderful resource hidden in the basement of the City of London Polytechnic in London's East End. The Women's Education Group (WedG) is experiencing funding problems and is unlikely to continue in its present form.

Finally, Dale Spender devotes a chapter to 'The Blank Future'. She argues for real change, for a move away from male control of education: 'When educationalists and teachers spend the same amount of time and care documenting and presenting women's version of experience as they do for men, when the world is described and explained from the point of view of women as well as men, and when both versions coexist in educational institutions, and are accorded equal validity, then the future for women will not be blank.'

An aspiration for the last decade of the second millenium.

Sue Adler
November 1988

Part One
The Old, Old Problem

Introduction: Schools cannot teach what society does not know

When Virginia Woolf analysed the English education system in 1938, in her book, *Three Guineas*, she concluded that there was no place in it for women, and that they would be better served by remaining *outsiders*, for while there were disadvantages in being outsiders, there were also benefits. Women could remain outside that patriarchal value system, transmitted without question — or intermission — and which was so destructive for men, as well as women, argued Woolf.

Forty-three years later, in February 1981, at a meeting of the Women's Education Group (WEdG), Annie Cornbleet addressed the same issue and indicated how little progress had been made. In outlining the education of schoolgirls, the realities and possibilities, in presenting information on the strain and struggle encountered by teachers who wish to question those patriarchal values and their transmission, and who wish to change the education system, Annie Cornbleet asked whether it was worth continuing. She asked whether it would be more realistic and more profitable for women to 'leave' education and to become outsiders.

This is a measure of the disenchantment that many women currently feel in relation to the education system, and it is disenchantment that is wholly justified.

For too long too many people have been prepared to accept that education is benign and neutral, that it is a 'good thing', and the more one gets the better off one will be. But feminists are among those who are seriously questioning this assumption and who are beginning to assert that *all* educational institutions embody a particular way of viewing the world, that *all* educational institutions require their students to adopt this world view, and that it is a limited, distorted and destructive framework for making sense of the world. Education, many feminists are arguing, is not at all a 'good thing' in its present form and, therefore, perhaps we would be better off without it.

That this may sound extreme is understandable, and it is a useful place to start, for this book is concerned with education in its broadest sense — with what we know in our society and how we come to know it — and it is interesting that we know so little that is critical of the fundamental principles and practices of education.

Gone are the days when we could believe that all knowledge existed 'out there', in the wilderness, merely waiting for brilliant men to 'discover' it and to make impartial records uncoloured by their own opinions and beliefs. Like it or not, we have to come to terms with more recent discoveries (to which feminism has made an enormous contribution) that human beings invent or construct knowledge in accordance with the values and beliefs with which they begin. What knowledge gets made, and what does not, why and how it is used, can provide much illumination about the people who have made it and the society in which they live. If there is little knowledge about oppressed groups, and if what there is portrays oppressed groups as inferior or incompetent, then it is perfectly reasonable to assume that those who are making the knowledge are not oppressed, and that they are not particularly interested in challenging the basis of oppression. Likewise, if there is little knowledge available about the inadequacies of education it is not unreasonable to assume that those who are making knowledge about education do not choose to look closely at its limitations. As a society, however, we are largely dependent on the knowledge they make (which includes the knowledge that we should defer to experts) and therefore, it is not surprising that we should use what we know and 'decide' that anyone who advocates leaving education is an extremist, and not to be taken seriously.

Such a response, however, tells us more about our own indoctrination and dependence (the 'success' of our own educational institutions) than it does about the merits of the case. We cannot trust what we know. It has been made and taught by individual human beings who have had (fallible) human reasons for making and teaching such knowledge, and we may or may not subscribe to those reasons. We need to ask ourselves *why* it is that we know what we know, and whose interests are being served.

Why do we know so little about women and blacks, for example, and why is so much of what we do know about them false, negative, and derogatory? Who has made this knowledge, on what basis and for what reasons? And why aren't these fundamental questions — which are so important — usually addressed in education institutions? Why is the substance of the curriculum almost exclusively white men (this is discussed in more detail later, see especially Part Two, The Knowledge of Males) and why, so often, does this go unnoticed or unchallenged? And why is it that the introduction of material on women and blacks is so frequently viewed as *political* when so much unmitigated nonsense on white men is given the stamp of approval, placed in halls of learning, is revered and called 'objective knowledge' and 'accumulated wisdom'?

These questions are fundamental to education, but they are questions which are rarely asked — particularly while education is controlled by white men. And because there is so little knowledge encoded on this topic, this is the place where I must begin (see Spender, 1981, b).

Schools cannot teach what society does not know, and while I am primarily interested in what is taught in schools, in why, and how, and with what results, I am obliged to begin with the limitations on knowledge. It is my contention that if sexism were to be removed from the curriculum there would be virtually nothing left to teach, because our society in general knows so little that is not sexist (see Spender, 1981). But such assertions require substantiation — such knowledge is not freely available and backed by a sanctified tradition — and so I have spent considerable time addressing the fundamental educational issue (not normally addressed by many educationalists) of what we know, and why.

Feminism has no choice but to take up this issue, for as Dorothy Smith (1978) has pointed out, most of what we know was constructed by men, and Ruth Hubbard (1981) has added that like all other human productions, knowledge — and in this case, the knowledge of science and biology — reflects 'the outlook and interests of the producers'. (Hubbard, 1981; p213). And, it seems, the subordination of women and blacks is very much in the interests of the producers (Jean Baker Miller, 1978), for much of their knowledge has been used to justify and reinforce such subordination (see Joan Roberts, 1976).

Scientists do not ask all possible questions, states Hubbard, only those which suit their methods and arouse their curiosity or interest (or the curiosity and interest of funding bodies) and what may arouse the curiosity or interest of socially and economically privileged university educated males may not be considered interesting by those who do not share their perspective. Conversely, what does not interest these men might well be a burning question to women. But the interests of men are pursued; knowledge is produced about men's interests and fed into the whole society, while the questions that may interest women too frequently 'evaporate' while men are in control.

Many feminists are beginning to claim that we can no longer afford to believe what we know, but must treat all that we know as suspect. There is no infallible way of finding the truth, of conducting value-free experiments and research, and providing objective results. Ruth

Hubbard has said that 'we find what we look for', that 'indeed, one can prove almost any hypothesis if one gets to set the terms of the experiment: to choose appropriate conditions, ask appropriate questions, select appropriate controls. And if one does a thorough job, the conclusion will have that quality of obviousness that scientists so enjoy at the end of meticulous research. And it really *is* obvious for it fits what we believe about the world: but the reason it fits so well is that it is founded on those very beliefs.' (p215). By this means we discovered the four humours of the body, leeching to cure disease — and those countless other cast-off truths, such as that women's brains would burst if they became educated. But the truths of today have also been 'discovered' by the same processes; the same privileged group of people have made them and they include the truths about the inferiority of oppressed groups. We can no longer afford to accept them.

In our current education system it is no longer necessary to make blatant racist and sexist statements in order to teach members of oppressed groups about their own inferiority and, hence, the 'justification' for their oppression. The issues can be managed in a much more detached manner. All that is needed is to present students with the idea that there is 'truth', and 'proven' and 'objective' knowledge, and then to teach them anything from history to biology, from literature to science, as they are presently constructed, and students will almost invariably learn that oppressed groups are inferior and therefore justifiably excluded from positions of influence and power.

The opportunities for resisting or repudiating this knowledge are limited indeed. First of all, if such knowledge *is* the truth, then there can be no point in protesting. Secondly, protests are likely to be perceived as *political* and if there is one area of knowledge that educationalists have created that has served them admirably, it is that education should be divorced from politics, that it should be impersonal: those who persistently ask why, for example, when there are so many possible versions of history, the only one considered 'proper' in most schools is 'white man's history', are likely to find themselves perceived as problems or politicos. And thirdly, there are so few 'ready-made' alternative bodies of knowledge available.

It simply is not possible for a fifteen-year-old girl, tired of hearing about men's wars in the nineteenth century, to confront the teacher with three possible alternative histories on the nineteenth century, viewed from the perspective of women, and to request that these books be included on the course. Even if such a fifteen-year-old did suspect that women had made just as much history as men but that men had chosen not to enter it in their records, even if she did suspect that the men's records would look very different if women, and not just men, were to comment on them, where could she find a collection of books to make her point?

Instead she will have to listen to a male record of male achievement in which implicitly and explicitly she is informed of the inferiority of women and if she refuses to accept this truth, then she engages in an act of faith, she defies the evidence (see Reuben, 1978).

This book is about *Knowledge and Control** and the role that the school plays in the process. It is not a book about sex stereotyping (I do not think the term arises throughout the book) for I do not believe that even a possible end to sex stereotyping would necessarily bring with it an end to oppression. There are societies where sex stereotyping is not as rigid as our own, even where it is the reverse of our own (see Margaret Mead, 1971, and Ann Oakley, 1972), but knowledge and control remain a comparable problem, for men are dominant and women are oppressed. Nor do I think sex stereotyping is a peculiar responsibility of the school — there is every reason to believe that girls were just as familiar with the role they were supposed to play, before they were allowed to attend schools, and today, I do not think it would be necessary to go to school to find out what is thought to be appropriately masculine and feminine in our culture.

My interest focuses on those people who helped to invent these sex roles and my curiosity is aroused when I find that it is men who have decreed what we know. We know, for example, that men have prestigious qualities such as reason, objectivity, leadership, independence, authority, while women have been allocated stigmatised qualities such as emotion, irrationality, passivity and dependence. Of course I am concerned at the wastefulness and the destructiveness of this division, but I am also concerned with its *convenience*. It puts men in the privileged position of continuing to create the knowledge of our society, of continuing to appropriate 'superiority' for themselves, to perpetuate patriarchy and to reinforce oppression.

When I pursue issues which interest me and arouse my curiosity (but which, unfortunately, do *not* usually arouse the interest or

*(A title used by Michael F.D. Young, 1975, and which I am sure he will 'lend' to me for my present purposes, despite the fact that his book makes few references to women).

curiosity of funding agencies which are controlled by men) I am doing nothing other than what men have done for centuries. I am engaged in the same process of constructing knowledge: I simply have a different perspective, which leads to different descriptions of education and schools, and different explanations. I do, however, make very different claims for what I know.

I do not seek to suggest — as men have so frequently done — that my view of education is the only view, that my descriptions and explanations are the one and only truth. My experience of the world is limited and this discussion is bound by those limitations. But this does not mean that my view is any less valid or credible than the conventional one, provided by men, which we have all been required to know in the past. While men have produced knowledge, one of their primary claims has been *vastness*: the knowledge which they have invented has often aimed to account for all people in all places at all times. In order to be considered sound, findings should be applicable to millions — even to the whole world —there should be order, and truth, and *universals*, in the reputable knowledge constructed by men.

I do not know if there are any universal truths: I can speak only from my own experience. I do want to know what sort of society seeks universals and devalues individual human experience.

While valuing and validating individual experience, however, I do not want to imply that there are no structures which influence and inhibit our ways of making sense of the world. It is those very structures that I want to describe and explain. For this reason many of the arguments in this book are equally applicable to all oppressed groups (and all oppressed groups include women) although the examples cited would change.

In this book I shall document the exclusion of women from knowledge produced by men, and while all men benefit from such knowledge, not all men have been equally represented in its construction. Blacks, working class people, old people, non-heterosexual people, disabled people could make exactly the same case as that made here for women. This is a book about power, about those who have the power to decide what we will know. The 'powerless' have had little choice but to accept not just the content, but the criteria of credibility. The 'powerless' can begin to make their own knowledge (we can begin by redefining ourselves) and in the process the present boundaries of knowledge, and control, will be drastically changed.

Currently, education and schools play a significant role in

constructing male supremacy and in perpetuating male dominance and control. This is why it is necessary to start with a description of that dominance and control. It may seem so pervasive, so deeply entrenched, that the possibility of dislodging patriarchal values could appear to be too remote to be realised. Some people may feel that there is no point in continuing within the present system. I know this is a possible interpretation.

But I also know that the foundations are fragile. I know that it doesn't take women nearly as long to learn that males are *not* superior, as it does to learn that they are. I know that thirty years of learning patriarchal values can be undermined in thirty seconds, and that the world never looks the same again. I know that women have been victims of an enormous hoax — and that it won't work twice. I know that women can be autonomous and that we are becoming so. I know that this can happen in schools. I do not think we should cease to be *outsiders* in the terms that Virginia Woolf used, but I think that we should become so strong and our concerns so central, that the term *outsider* is no longer appropriate.

1 There's Nothing New About Sexism

Protests about Sexism and Education are not new: for over three hundred years many women and some men have protested about the way men have organised education in the interest of men and at the expense of women. While the examples have sometimes changed from one century to the next, the understandings and the accusations have remained constant: men have controlled education and have ordained that males shall receive preferential treatment.

When it comes to documenting the history of women's protest about male control of education, there are many places where we could begin. We could go back to Virginia Woolf, who in 1928 wrote a searing critique of men's education, entitled *Three Guineas*. Or we could go back to Harriet Martineau (1800-1872), one of the first political economists and a woman who understood the implications of different education for the different sexes; or Mary Somerville (1780-1872), a leading scientist of her day who knew from bitter experience about male control of education. Or we could begin with Mary Wollstonecraft, who in 1792 published *A Vindication of the Rights of Woman* in which the responsibility for creating a 'superior' sex is placed squarely upon men who have used education to this end. There is 'Sophia, A Person of Quality' who in 1739 published *Woman not Inferior to Man: or, short and modest Vindication of the Natural Right of the Fair Sex to a perfect Equality of Power, Dignity and Esteem with the Men*; in her pamphlet she asserted that education was one of the major means used by men to advance their superiority over women, and she argued that if women were permitted the same educational advantages as men they would soon expose and eliminate the ostensible superiority of men.

However, I am going to begin with Aphra Behn (1640-1689) partly because in the last couple of years we have come to know a great deal more about her, and partly because the case she made in the seventeenth century, against male control of education, is still applicable today.

As Angeline Goreau (1980) has stated, Aphra Behn led an extraordinary life. She was not a woman of wealth or rank but in her lifetime she made a trip to the West Indies where she became involved in a slave rebellion. She was a spy for Charles II and was imprisoned for debt — partly because of the expenses she incurred in her service for the King. She was a feminist who demanded autonomy for women and, of course, full educational rights. Angeline Goreau says of her that 'She was an early abolitionist whose novel *Oroonoko* contained the first popular portrayal of the horrors of slavery . . . she was a writer who not only insisted on being heard, but who successfully forced the men who dominated the jealous literary world of Restoration England to recognise her as an equal. In a London that boasted only two theaters, she had seventeen plays produced in seventeen years. She wrote thirteen novels (thirty years before Daniel Defoe wrote *Robinson Crusoe*, generally termed [by the male dominated literary establishment] the first novel) and published several collections of poems and translations.' (Goreau, 1980; pp3-4).

Though it was not labelled *sexism*, she frequently addressed the issue of what we today would call *sexism and education* in her literary and dramatic work. One of the reasons that she commented so frequently and fervently on women's education was because the men of the literary establishment of the time criticised her not just because she was a woman, and a successful woman — although such criticism was frequent enough — but because she did not know Latin and Greek, an understanding of which was then considered to be the necessary sign of 'an educated man'.

Aphra Behn was justifiably furious because these critics were the very same men who would not allow women to learn Latin or Greek (on the scientific grounds that their brains would burst or that they would become unfit for child-bearing) and she exposed their hypocrisy, and their motives, in much of her work. Again and again she demonstrated that men controlled education, that they prevented women from learning, and then condemned women because they were ignorant.

The men of Aphra Behn's time could not dispute her enormous success, but they could attempt to demean her achievement, and this some of them did by insisting on their own superiority, their own authority to decree what was good and what was not. Her plays were not very good, they were not up to the proper standard, argued many of the male critics, because they could not possibly be based on any understanding of the ancient classics.

This was something which Aphra Behn could not ignore. In her writing, which reached a wide audience, she challenged these men.

She demolished their arguments and exposed the absurdities, and injustices, of the education system which men had set up and which practised preferential treatment for men.

Like many contemporary women who wish to see women possess the same educational resources as men, Aphra Behn was not content to urge that women should simply learn Latin and Greek like men; she did not assume that the male way was the right way. On the contrary she turned the argument round and pointed out that Latin and Greek were not necessary qualifications for writing literature, only for membership of an exclusive male club. 'We all well know' she said 'that the immortal Shakespeare's plays (who was not guilty of much more of this [classical learning] than often falls to women's share) have better pleased the world than Johnson's works': and he *did* know Latin and Greek. (From 'Epistle to the Reader' quoted in Goreau, 1980; p135). Men, argued Aphra Behn, were simply using a knowlege of Latin and Greek as a pretext for asserting their superiority.

Men would not acknowledge the equal abilities of women, and even when presented with evidence that women were competent — indeed, could excel in areas that they had reserved for themselves — men found ways of dismissing women's contributions. When confronted with damning criticism after the successful performance of her play *Sir Patient Fancy*, she wrote in the preface to the printed version that 'the play had no other misfortune but that of coming out for a woman's' and 'had it been owned by a man, though the most dull unthinking rascally scribbler in town, it had been a most admirable play.' (Quoted in Goreau, 1980; p233).

This learning that men devised for themselves, and confined to themselves, was merely a convenient peg on which to hang the excuse that women could not be as capable as men, no matter what women did, argued Aphra Behn. She added that if the men who criticised her were examples of what happened to the intellect after learning Latin and Greek, then women would probably be better off without men's learning, for it by no means encouraged the development of a fair and open mind, or an understanding of human beings.

She ridiculed her literary colleagues and 'the ponderous logic and pretentious language that academic pronouncements on drama were couched in' (Goreau, 1980; p132) and even lampooned certain members of the Royal Society, and, of course, all these targets for her satire were males. She revealed what men were doing, and why, in the name of education and learning. Defiantly sarcastic, Aphra Behn first of all refused to be intimidated into a sense of inferiority because of the ignorance of her sex (an ignorance carefully cultivated by men) and secondly she persistently dismissed 'the much vaunted "learning" that *she* (had) been denied as so much "academic frippery" '.(p133).

For at least 300 years women have been making the same protest as Aphra Behn. They have been pointing to the dimension of power and control in education and have been showing the way that men use their influence in education to decree the standards and to ensure that they favour men. Many women have demanded not just equal access to the education that men have deemed important, not just a chance to try to meet the standards set by men on the basis of men's experience, but equal access to the decision making processes about what form education is to take, what is to be important, what standards are to be set.

For while men are the policy and decision makers, while education remains under male control and men decide what is important, we will not know about Aphra Behn and the many women before and after her; every generation will be led to believe that sexism and education is something new. We are kept in ignorance (as were our predecessors) with the result that we constantly have to assert that such ignorance is not of our own making, to resist being intimidated into accepting our own inferiority, to demonstrate that men's learning does not encompass many of the values that we deem important. We have been stating our case for centuries, but without continuity.

I have started with Aphra Behn because the charges she made three hundred years ago are, in many respects, as applicable today as they were then. But I have also introduced Aphra Behn because she is one of the casualties of sexist education. The fact that she is virtually unknown today while some of her less successful male colleagues are part of the established tradition (Wycherly for example had only three plays performed, she had seventeen) is an example of one of the consequences of male control. It is not knowledge of Latin and Greek that we are deprived of today, it is knowledge about women like Aphra Behn. We have been kept in ignorance about the protests that women have made so that every generation has to begin again from the beginning. The understandings that women have forged do not constitute a discipline or a subject, they are not systematically encoded and transmitted to the next generation; it is men who monopolise the influential positions from which it is decided what is to be taught.

We are deprived of our knowledge, our heritage, our learning, we are required to become familiar with knowledge encoded by men and about men, and we are asked to accept that this is *all* that there is, that this is the sum total of human knowledge. Under the circumstances it is not surprising that we should (erroneously) conclude that we have made a new discovery when we locate and identify the way in which education and learning has been used to structure and support male supremacy. It is a mark of our sexist education system that we could believe that sexism in education is something new and that three hundred years at least of women's protest and struggle could be kept out of the record without our knowledge or consent.

Part Two
The Knowledge of Males

2 Off the Record

The Problem of Men

Many people today react — as they did in Aphra Behn's time — by declaring these charges against men as unfair, unjust, unsubstantiated — even outrageous. This is not at all surprising because the understandings forged by women over the last three hundred years and more have played no part in any conventional educational curriculum. It is quite difficult to accept that for centuries there has been a substantial and growing body of knowledge which has *not* made its presence felt in education because it would challenge and undermine the power of those who are in control. To recognise that this body of knowledge does exist is also to recognise that we have probably been victims of indoctrination, rather than education, and such an insight can be quite disturbing, particularly when we have also been frequently taught that we are a privileged society being presented with the *full* facts and not a partial or prejudiced view of the facts.

That we know little or nothing about women's traditions is directly related to the male control of education, for the problems of education are the problems that are decreed by men, and women's exclusion and disadvantage has not figured as a problem for men. While generation after generation of women has protested — often vehemently and to a wide audience — their words have 'disappeared' and this process continues to the present day. The process helps to maintain and perpetuate male control, and it is necessary to understand it, and the way it works, if we are to understand sexism and education.

In our society it is men who have been and who are the 'authorities' on every aspect of existence — including those aspects that are seen as women's prerogatives, such as child development (for example, Dr Spock). Some of the 'reasons' that have been put forward to justify the prominence of men are quite remarkable. One of the most common is that women are inferior — because they are women. This inferiority has been 'proved' in numerous ways which range from their brains being smaller (or larger) to women being ruled by a mysterious force such as their instincts, or their hormones. The 'proof' has changed over the centuries but the necessity for establishing the inferiority of women has remained much the same. Because women have not been among the 'great' that we have learnt about in our educational institutions, then many educationalists (and scientists and psychologists and politicians, *etc.*) have taken this as evidence that women are indeed inferior.

But how accurate is this evidence? Who has chosen and selected it, and what does it ignore? Aphra Behn knew the answer to this: she knew that the crucial omission from this explanation was the factor of male control. She knew that men had prevented her from acquiring certain knowledge and skills and had then blamed her because she did not possess them. Mary Astell (1694) knew, when in *A Serious Proposal to the Ladies* she said 'Women are from their very infancy debarred those advantages of education with the want of which they are afterwards reproached.' And Mary Wollstonecraft (1792) knew, for she wrote a book almost entirely about the problem (*A Vindication of the Rights of Woman*). Women's understandings, however, have not been incorporated into our cultural heritage, with the result that men have continued to explain the absence of women from the record in terms of women, and not in terms of men. While the subject of male control has for centuries been a problem for women, it has never presented a serious problem for men, with the result that they have not addressed the topic and have often dismissed the whole area as unimportant and insignificant — and they have been in the position to have their assessment accepted by women as well as men.

For women, however, male dominance has always been a problem, and when women begin to explain the absence of women from the record, they do so from a very different perspective and with very different results. Within the tradition of Aphra Behn, Mary Wollstonecraft and Virginia Woolf, Dorothy Smith (1978) is one of the more recent to describe and explain how the exclusion of women has been achieved in a male dominated society. Men, she says, have attended to and treated as significant only what men say. 'The circle of men whose writing and talk was significant to each other extends backwards in time as far as our records reach. What men were doing was relevant to men, was written by men about men for men. Men listened and listen to what one another said.' (Smith, 1978; p281).

This is how a tradition is formed, 'as the circle of those present builds on the work of the past. From these circles women have been excluded or admitted only by a special licence granted to a woman as

...ver as a representative of her sex.' (p281). ...understandings have been kept out, and when ...y there are no women represented in the culture's ...owledge, men have argued that there are no women ...have had nothing to contribute.

...s: 'The universe of ideas, images and themes — the sy... ...es which are *the general currency* of thought — have been either p......ced by men or controlled by them. In so far as women's work and experience has been entered into it, it has been on terms decided by men and because it has been approved by men .... This is why women have had no written history until very recently, no share in making religious thoughts, no political philosophy, no representations of society from their view, no poetic tradition, no tradition in art.' (p282).

It is not that women have not played an equal part in history, but that men have written the history books and have focused on the problems of men: it is not that women have not generated religious thoughts, formulated political philosophies, explained society, written poetry or been artists, but that men have controlled the records for religion, philosophy, politics, poetry and art and they have concentrated on the contributions of men (see Lynne Spender, *Unpublished Heritage: The Politics of Selection*; in press).

This problem of male control, which is so obvious in its *absence* from the male records, runs right through the writing of women. It is a crucial concern of contemporary feminism. Men have provided us with a false picture of the world, argues Mary Daly (1973), not just because their view is so limited, but because they have insisted that their *limited* view is the *total* view. They have insisted that their *male* experience of the world is the *human* experience, and this has necessitated denying the experience of women where it is different from the experience of men. Women have raised the problem, again and again, but because it is not a problem of male experience, men have dismissed it.

Elizabeth Janeway (1980) is another contemporary feminist concerned with this problem and she outlines it in her book, *Powers of the Weak*. All the meanings, understandings, knowledge, we have available to us in our society, she argues, are produced by those in power, by those who do the governing, 'while the governed rest of us are pretty well ignored' (p3); the meanings, understandings and knowledge that we forge in our daily lives are dismissed. We, the governed, know what the world looks like from the position of the dominants — for their view has been imposed on us as *the* view of society — but neither we, nor they, have systematic and coherent understandings about the nature of the world as a whole, which would necessarily include the experience of women, for as subordinates we are excluded (by definition) from those circles in which social knowledge is constructed, and we are isolated with our meanings, unable to articulate them for each other, or for men.

The problem is that the problems of men are only *half* the human problems. They constitute a one-sided view of the world and this encourages the construction of limited and distorted explanations (including the explanation that women are not among the 'greats' of our culture — which in turn 'proves' that women are inferior). Jean Baker Miller (1976) writes 'Until recently, "mankind's" understandings have been the only understandings generally available to us. As other perceptions arise — precisely those perceptions that men because of their dominant position could *not* perceive — the total vision of human possibilities enlarges and is transformed. The old is severely challenged.' (p1).

From the position of subordination women can see that men miss much of the evidence and can construct only poorly informed explanations: women know a great deal about the world that men do ✱not, they know a great deal about men that men do not know about themselves, and until women's view of the world coexists with men's view of the world, our entire system of education will be limited, distorted, sexist. Women have a responsibility to describe the world from the position they occupy — for other women; and for men, who will not know unless they are informed. If we wish to describe and analyse *human* experience, and to formulate explanations of the world which take *human beings* into account, then we must include the experience and understandings of women, as well as men.

Without benefit of a record or a tradition women have had to find out for themselves as Aphra Behn did. While men take it for granted that they can build on what has gone before, selecting, refining, adapting the knowledge they have inherited to meet their needs, women are constantly required to begin with a blank sheet. We can even find it remarkable that Catherine Macaulay wrote a book on women's education (*Letters on Education*) in 1790 which assumed that sex differences could be accounted for in terms of socialisation (particularly education) and that the 'natural' superiority of men was not natural at all but a product of their own control and 'engineering'. Mary Wollstonecraft read and reviewed that book and when she wrote her own book in 1792 acknowledged her deep debt to Catherine Macaulay: how much more might she — and Macaulay

— have done if they had been part of a known long line of women benefiting from the insights of those who had gone before, instead of a small 'episode' which materialises and then disappears?

While males control education there is no direct means for women to pass on their understandings. What women know frequently dies with them, until feminists periodically rediscover them and their writing and attempt to reconstruct women's heritage and tradition. Each generation of women forges understandings about subordination, within their own lifetime and from the circumstances of their own lives, but because these meanings do not become the general currency of the culture they are not passed on to the next generation with the result that neither women nor men know about the women who have gone before.

So when men argue that male dominance is not a problem, that women have nothing to protest about, that there is no sexism in education, they are simply asserting — and quite rightly — that from their point of view it is *not* a problem. If women's point of view were equally valued — which it is not — we could just agree to differ, and attribute our different explanations to different experience. But women are subordinates — our view does not count as much as men's. It is men who have a problem, for they see little and assume they see all, they assume their experience is human experience — but human beings are not merely male.

The Disappearance of Women

When we examine what is presented to us as *our* cultural heritage and traditions, there can be no disagreement about the role played by women within it, for they are simply not there. It is their very *absence* from the record that is so obvious. But where disagreement can arise is in terms of what this absence means, and how and why it has occurred.

We could assume that males are superior and explain the absence of women by arguing that it was impossible for women to reach the high standards set by men with the result that no women have been worthy of inclusion in the male record. This is the way many people do argue, probably because they do not know anything about Aphra Behn and her successors.

But what if we do know about Aphra Behn, about the scientists Mary Somerville and Hertha Ayrton, about political journalists from Mary Manley (1663-1724) to Harriet Martineau, about Catherine Macaulay and Mary Wollstonecraft, and the many hundreds of other 'unknown' women whose names would probably be meaningless? What if we do know about the enormous contributions that these women have made, the reputations they have enjoyed in their own lifetimes, but which have since 'disappeared'?

That these women are not mentioned within our own education does not prove to us that they do not exist, instead it begins to suggest that there is something wrong with our education and the knowledge that is transmitted within it. Once we have begun to find out about these women it is perfectly reasonable that we should become suspicious about their omission. We are being nothing less than sensible when we start to look more closely at the male records and nothing less than logical when we make connections between male control of education, an exclusive focus on the behaviour of males, and the claim — and evidence — that males are the superior sex.

We can turn to virtually any branch of knowledge and show how men have 'written off' women so that they disappear, and what we know about women's education in the past is but one example. History, said Virginia Woolf in 1929, is the history of the male line, and the history of education, argues Margaret Bryant (1979), is no exception, for it is the history of men's education. While for centuries women have demanded education, and while during the nineteenth century there was a revolution when they achieved many of their demands (such as entry to the universities), this goes virtually unreported in the literature. If treated at all, the history of women's education is usually 'a separate aspect of specialist educational history' (p17) and *not* the history of the majority of the population. For those who may doubt the extent of the disappearance of women, the enormity of the male 'bias', Margaret Bryant suggests they consult 'the index of almost any general survey of nineteenth-century British history published recently' (p18) where they will find almost a complete absence of any reference to women despite the vast revolutionary changes and upheavals (and the bitter resistance to them) that took place. At Cambridge, for example, a great battle was waged over women's entry to the university — a battle that continues, but in which one victory was won in 1948 when women were permitted to become full members of the university (see Rita McWilliams-Tullberg, 1975). The establishment of the women's colleges of Newnham and Girton was accompanied by bitter recriminations and dire warnings of gloom and doom, but the book *Revolution of the Dons: Cambridge and Society in Victorian England* (1968) 'has nothing to say about women'. (Bryant, 1979; p18).

The process of making women disappear — no matter what their achievements — continues to the present day. As a result women are unable to perceive themselves as part of a tradition: we presume we are without predecessors and believe we must start from the beginning because we have no knowledge of what has gone before. We have no 'education' of our own regardless of the number of institutions we attend or the qualifications we collect. We are not permitted the opportunity of learning from our past, of developing and refining our heritage (which is something which men take for granted for themselves), but instead, have our confidence and self-esteem systematically undermined, until we become doubtful and dubious about ourselves and our lives, and are prepared to believe the myths of our man-made inferiority for lack of evidence to the contrary. We accept the explanation provided by men that women have nothing of value to contribute to our culture.

Conveniently, we are also denied the knowledge of the history of men's reaction to our demands. There are no books by the (male) historians, educationalists, philosophers, psychologists, sociologists, *etc.*, which trace the unsavoury history of the absurd and hostile arguments men have resorted to, in order to keep women in their place. A history of women's education would have to include some coverage of male resistance, and far from supporting the idea of male supremacy, and showing men in a good light, this would often reveal the mean and petty lengths (as well as the exploitative and savage lengths) to which some men have been prepared to go in order to retain and maintain their control over women. The history of men's reasons for keeping women out of education would provide a very enlightening read.

For example, we could begin with Jean-Jacques Rousseau, one of the founding fathers of modern education, who believed that women were created for the purpose of entertaining and caring for men, and that their education should equip them for the task. 'Woman is made to please and to be in subjection to man.' he stated, and 'she ought to make herself pleasing to his eyes'. Because her education should be directed towards making her attractive to men, Rousseau created Sophie to serve as an example of what it was necessary for a young girl to know, in order to become an ideal wife. Women must be confined and restrained, he argued, urged to practise self-sacrifice in order to acquire that 'docility which woman requires all her life long, for she will always be in subjection to a man, or to a man's judgement and she will never be free to set her own opinion above his.'

In making up his theories it is very easy to perceive how Rousseau was concerned with promoting the interests of men. He asserted that women were naturally dependent, disinclined to learn, and silly, and, therefore, according to the rules of *his logic*, they should be given little or no opportunity to be independent, to acquire knowledge, or to become better informed. With men's interests at heart, he argued that it was best for men if women were to be mindless coquettes, and with considerable enthusiasm he set about developing a system that would turn them into mindless coquettes. The same old argument — he denied women the knowledge that men had access to, and then blamed them for their 'inadequacies'; he also preposterously described the whole business as the unfolding of nature.

Mary Wollstonecraft called him to account and exposed the absurdities and fallacies of his case, but it would not be in the interests of men for Rousseau's deficiencies or Wollstonecraft's analysis of them to become common knowledge, and so this aspect of his theory and her exposé were quickly dropped. As Sheila Ruth (1980) points out, 'It is a measure of the extent and pervasiveness of sexism (male control) in our culture, and in the history of ideas, that Rousseau's happy acceptance of the enslavement of more than half the human race does not interfere with his reputation as a champion of liberty'. (p115).

This is because, for men, that is how he appears; for as the enslavement of women did not present a problem to many men, it has gone unnoticed, and men have been free to continue to impose on women an education that is designed to make them more 'attractive' to men, rather than to develop the potential of women. As Herbert Spencer (1861), another founding father, said, 'Men care little for erudition in women' (p187) so they have devised a system which helps to prevent women explicitly and implicitly from acquiring it.

In the past the provisions have been much more explicit and women have been physically prevented from attending places of learning (in contrast with some of the more implicit contemporary practices which prevent women from acquiring knowledge about women), and many and various have been the justifications for this practice. One fundamental objection that men put forward was that women would be desexed if they were to be educated, and that if they had any other options, they might even find the prospect of marriage insufficiently attractive for them to enter into it. Carol Dyhouse (1976) has helped to remind us of the male fears and arguments that have been used to deny education to women, but because today these arguments are so often patently ridiculous, they do not constitute information that men want to publicise about themselves. So this record of male behaviour has also disappeared in the main from the male record.

Many men were frightened, says Carol Dyhouse, that allowing women greater access to education would mean an end to male control and privilege, and among them 'There were ... those who felt that education, particularly in its secondary or higher forms, was rendering women physiologically unfit for motherhood. This argument took various forms — some exponents emphasising their conviction that educated women were reduced to infertility, or unable to breastfeed their children, the majority expressing their anxiety about the physiological implications of overstrain or mental fatigue. Secondly, there were a large number ... who believed that educational arrangements as they existed, both at the elementary and higher levels, were calculated to disincline women from the prospect of motherhood as a worthwhile or sufficient goal in life. This latter school tended to add their voices to the loud if ill-assorted chorus of theorists and polemicists who predicted, with gloomy certitude, the decline of the family and moral ties . . .' (p44).

Today we are told (as women were told then) that women's entry to positions which males have reserved for themselves, will be accompanied by a decline in the family, a collapse of moral values, that women will grow hairs on their chests (a recent finding from Cambridge University) and lose their femininity. What we are *not* told is that men have been saying this for centuries, as a means of trying to scare women off, and as a means of protecting their own privilege. This is the knowledge which 'disappears'.

Herbert Spencer (1876) said that it would be mischievous to allow women to enter education and paid work on the same basis as men, for they would no longer be content to carry out the tasks that men had allocated to them (such as looking after men). Others argued that if women engaged in sedentary studies it would result in pelvic distortion that could complicate the birth process, and there was the common 'conviction that anything above a minimal level of intellectual effort would overstrain the constitution of the average woman, and be very likely to result in infertility, inhibit lactation, or even induce serious mental disturbance.' (Dyhouse, 1976; p44). Dorothea Beale (1868) had to expose the stupidities of these arguments in exactly the same way as did her predecessor Mary Wollstonecraft — but this is not part of the record.

In the first decade of the twentieth century Dr Murray Leslie supported 'the contention that hockey-playing could very easily deprive girls of the ability to breastfeed in later life' and he was further convinced 'that intellectual pursuits increased the chances of psychiatric disorder among women.' (Dyhouse, 1976; p46). Whereas men could choose to be educated and to enter paid employment without penalty, it was put to women that if they availed themselves of even some of the limited opportunities that were permitted them, they did so at great risk. Women were hardly encouraged by men to develop their own potential, and many came to believe these man-made myths that they would become mentally or physically ill if they ventured into male preserves, and a number therefore decided — as intended by many men — that it was not worth the risk.

Women are still warned today, still discouraged from entering education and employment on the same basis as men, and still presented with 'proof' that their own health and that of their families will suffer if they do not stay in their proper place which men have defined for them. They are still encouraged to pursue an education that will make them attractive to men, who still frequently find erudition in women intimidating, and therefore unattractive and undesirable. One of the most influential educationalists of the last few decades, John Newsom, constantly urged that women's education should be designed to fit them as wives and mothers, as homemakers for their husbands and children, that they should 'relearn the graces that so many had forgotten.' (Newsom, 1948). If women had known that this was the same old line that men had been using for centuries, *and that women had been discrediting for centuries*, and exposing as the ruse for the perpetuation of male privilege, they would have been in a much better position to resist these arguments.

Men have bowed to the pressure of women and have opened up many institutions and subjects to women, but men remain decidedly in control of the institutions and the subjects, and are able to determine what women will learn. And women do not learn much about the value and the strength of women. On the contrary, now that women do have access to many areas of men's education, women are learning more comprehensively and systematically about the value and significance of men, for men have ensured that women have 'disappeared' in the knowledge which is presented.

Women learn that they are not as worthy, that they do not count as much, and that what competence they may have is usually restricted to a specialised sphere which does not rank highly in the male scheme of values. They learn that there are territories that are reserved for men and that they enter these only at great risk. They often learn that it is more sensible to accept what they are taught, to believe in their own inadequacy and inferiority than to defy the evidence constructed by men.

So men continue to dominate and to use their influential positions to make women disappear. And they continue to use the absence of women as a justification for their own supremacy. Unlike their predecessors who were left exposed by charges that women were *actively* prevented from engaging in the same learning activities as men, many today may self-righteously assert that, within the disciplines they have established, there are no institutional barriers against women's entry.

But there is something missing from this 'explanation'. One of the things men fail to mention is that they have never established a discipline in which women's concerns are central and fundamental: they have never generated an area of knowledge that records women's perspective and women's strength. And this is an *omission* which allows them to reap many benefits, for without such a discipline it is not necessary to erect impediments to women's participation in men's disciplines, without such a discipline women can come to believe that the world of science, for example, is not for them. Women were kept out of Latin and Greek because men explicitly refused them entry: they are kept out of science by more sophisticated 'magic' which denies their existence (Kelly, 1981). Both methods have been equally effective in ensuring that men continue to dominate — for very good reasons supplied by men.

Keeping women out

Women have been kept 'off the record' in most, if not all, branches of knowledge by the simple process of men naming the world as it appears to them.* They have taken themselves as the starting point, defined themselves as central, and then proceeded to describe the rest of the world in relation to themselves. They have assumed their experience is universal, that it is representative of humanity, and that it constitutes a basis for generalising about *all* human beings. Whenever the experience of women is different from men, therefore, it stays 'off the record', for there is no way of entering it into the record when the experience is not shared by men, and men are the ones who write the record.

It is because of this process that we are daily confronted with many confusing and contradictory meanings. Men, for example, have

*For a more extensive coverage of the disciplines see Dale Spender (Ed), 1981, *Men's Studies Modified: the impact of feminism on the academic disciplines*, Pergamon Press, Oxford.

defined what they do as work, and where women do not do the same things as men, they are classified as *not* working, regardless of the number of hours they spend engaged in physical chores. A woman who may spend more than twelve to fifteen hours per day (seven days a week) in cleaning, cooking and caring for children, who may have interrupted nights and demanding days in which there are no rest periods, can find herself saying 'Oh, I don't work. I'm only a housewife.' This demonstrates the male monopoly on meaning, for in the face of overwhelming evidence to the contrary, such women have learned to deny the realities of their own life (in which they work harder and longer than men in general, according to the UN statistics) and to take on the male definitions of the world in which the only *real* work that is performed, is undertaken by men.

And because it is not work that women are engaged in, in servicing their husbands and children, then of course, it does not require payment.

Such servicing rapidly becomes work and requires payment if it is not undertaken by the wife/mother, and as Gerda Lerner (1977) has pointed out, few are the men who could afford to pay for their own servicing, and even a half share of the servicing of their children. 'The housewife does indeed work' states Gerda Lerner, and 'what is the value of her work in economic terms? Economists of the Chase Manhattan Bank of New York have recently calculated that the thirty million American women, who do not work outside the home and who list their occupations as "housewives", are each doing unpaid work worth $257.53 a week on the current labor market. The work they do includes twelve different skills categories. Each of the services the housewife performs becomes a legitimate paid occupation when performed by men in the market place . . . The aggregate of houswives' services amounts to $250 billion a year, which would be a sizeable portion of the GNP, if it were in it. That these staggering sums are a conservative estimate is indicated by the fact that they do not include the childrearing services rendered by housewives, nor do they include the housework of those women who work outside of the home, but who are also part time housewives.' (p110).

The maintenance of daily life and the rearing of children are absolutely fundamental to any society, but in our own, men have foisted the daunting task upon women, have denied that it constitutes work, have made it no part of their sciences of sociology or economics to name but a few, and have required that women do all this for love. Under the circumstances the fear that women might not choose to be wives and mothers, that they might even remain independent of men if any other options were available to them, is probably justified.

Because men have kept the work of women off the record, branches of knowledge such as economics and sociology, for example, have been built upon very distorted premises. In economics, the necessary and critical work that women perform is not taken into account — even when it constitutes the source of food. Women's work in the Himalayan region includes 70% of the agricultural work, in Africa 60-80%, and rural women in developing countries as a whole account for at least 50% of the food production (UN statistics) but this is not included in the economic analysis. *When the same jobs are performed by men, they count as work.*

So women and men, virtually the world over, learn that women do not work, no matter how much work women do, because women and their work are kept off the record. We even accept without question the ridiculous cliché that during the Industrial Revolution work was taken out of the home!

This is the knowledge that is constructed and disseminated in our society and it is the very core of sexist education that women have their lives and their work repudiated, while men control knowledge and its distribution. Women are required to take on men's definitions of the world, which enhance the image and increase the value of men, and in the process women are required to deny their own experience, to accept men's definitions of them as inferior, to believe that they are less valuable, and to collaborate in the business of keeping women off the record. And the dependence of one sex, emotionally and financially, on the other, gets constructed.

For example, sociology, which is supposed to be the study of society, is as Jessie Bernard (1973) has pointed out the male study of male society. Just as male historians have studied the activities of men, so too have male sociologists studied the activities of men. In her book, *The Sociology of Housework*, Ann Oakley (1974) has said that women are invisible in sociology, that women are 'concealed' in everything from 'the classification of subject areas and the definition of concepts through the topics and methods of empirical research to the construction of models and theory generally.' (p3).

Under male control, sociology has developed a classification scheme and a set of concepts which automatically exclude women, because they pertain to the activities of men. Sociologists, for example, have elected to focus on power, on the exercise of power through politics, the law, business, *etc.*, and as Oakley says 'these are the male dominated arenas' and 'the more sociology is concerned with such areas, the less it is, by definition, likely to include women within its framework of reference.' (p4). Sociology has developed a classification scheme for evaluating the socio-economic status of members of society, but it is a classification scheme based on men and is not applicable to women — which does not of course prevent sociologists from using it in relation to women.

Socio-economic status as devised by male controlled sociology, is based on the family unit, and assumes that all members of the family share the same status — that of the man. For lots of reasons this is a somewhat foolish assumption which has to be 'wrong' far more often than 'right', but which serves to keep women off the record and to make them and their contribution invisible. One objection to these assumptions is that in our society the nuclear family unit is a minority arrangement, and more people live in alternative households than in the nuclear family, so the classification scheme, from the outset, applies to only less than half the population. But perhaps the reason that its 'inadequacies' are tolerated is because it can disguise the fact that women have resources of their own. When it is assumed that only the man has status, the resources of women are rendered invisible — their wealth (however small), their pay, their education, their occupational training, are all wiped away with one stroke, for they do not count in determining the socio-economic status of the family. If we were to look at women's resources many would emerge in a very different class from their husbands (as Mrs Thatcher could testify, for example) but the system is cleverly arranged so that even Mrs Thatcher's resources could be denied and her status determined by her husband.

When students come to learn about economics or sociology (or language, literature, education, psychology, philosophy, political science, anthropology, science) they are taught about men, and men's view of the world, and this is a lesson in male supremacy. While on the one hand women have achieved some success in gaining entry to education, it is entry to men's education and it serves to reinforce male supremacy and control in our society.

Economists, for example, have expended an enormous amount of energy in constructing their explanations, their models and theories, but because they are concerned with men, they have only half the evidence in their possession (which might be one of the reasons for their lack of success). When women structure explanations about 'economics' they do so from different premises and they come up with different understandings. Lisa Leghorn and Kathy Parker (1981) have said that the world over, women produce leisure for men! Such 'insights' do not come readily to men, for whom the production of such leisure goes often unnoticed and unacknowledged, and never figures in their economic theory. (How many male economists produce their theories in the leisure time made available to them by women? How many women help research, draft, type and edit these theories, along with providing the meals, doing the washing and cleaning, all of which remains invisible and does not count in the schemata of economics?)

As far as men are concerned it is seen as just that those who work should be paid — if they are men. They have even written their economic histories to show how we, as a society, are supposed to have moved to a monetary economy where work is paid for. But they have completely omitted any consideration of women's work, it figures not at all in their theories and explanation, for 'In a money economy' states Gerda Lerner (1977) 'it is the only job offering no pay, but like indentured servitude (a thing of the past in male experience) support in exchange for services.' (p108).

And what are some of the consequences of denying women's work and thereby being able to insist that it goes unpaid? One of the consequences is that men are able to amass financial resources —99% of the world's wealth — and with less than 1% available to women, it is not surprising to find that for women there is not enough to go round. They must turn to men and become economically dependent on men. Moreover their finances are often only forthcoming while they cultivate the goodwill of men, and accept the enhanced image of men projected by many men.

Economics and sociology are not the only, or even the main, culprits in this attempt to keep women off the record, and practitioners of education have been busy in promoting and substantiating the belief that men are more important, their behaviour more significant, and their education more crucial. The records of educational sociology present such a distorted picture, states Sandra Acker (1980), that anyone who used them as a guide to the practices of our society would arrive at rather strange interpretations, for they 'would conclude that numerous boys but few girls go to secondary modern schools; that there are no girls' public schools; that there are almost no adult influentials of any sort; that most students in higher education study science and engineering; that women rarely make a ritual transition called "from school to work" and never go into further education colleges. Although some women go to university, most probably enter directly into motherhood where they are of some interest as transmitters of language codes to their children. And except for a small number of teachers, social workers and nurses, there are almost no adult women workers in the labour market.' (p5).

Within education more knowledge is made about men, more importance is attached to their education and more significance given to their experience, and this is the discipline which influences and even determines the parameters of education in schools and colleges. In surveying publications in the sociology of education since 1960, Sandra Acker reports that 37% of them were concerned exclusively with males while only 5% were concerned exclusively with women, and this does not satisfactorily document the extent of the male 'bias', for among the 5% concerned with women were studies that focused not on women as autonomous individuals (as was the case with men) but as transmitters of a code to young children. And of the 58% of studies in which the sex of the subjects was not specifically stated, it would be unwise to assume that both sexes were included: many of them could well have been about males, but so common is the practice of focusing on males that it was not thought necessary to make this explicit.

One hundred years ago women were not permitted entry to certain buildings, access to certain teachers, the opportunity to use certain resources which were the province of education; today, because they are allowed to enter the buildings, interact with the teachers, and make use of the materials, many assume, and some are prepared to assert, that the sexes have achieved educational equality, that there is no problem of male control and no issue of female exclusion. But education is a great deal more than buildings, teachers and materials; it is also about the knowledge that is learnt within these institutions, and in many respects women have gained little or nothing over the last one hundred — or even three hundred — years. We are in a similar position to Aphra Behn, in that men control the knowledge that is made available within the walls by the teachers and through the resources, and it is controlled so that women are kept off the record. We learn virtually nothing about our own lives, we are provided with little or no understanding about our existence, we are allowed few if any insights about out past, we receive no evidence of our autonomy or strength and we are denied any knowledge which would encourage us to develop independently of men. We are made to feel inferior by the education we are given and then blamed for our inferiority: we are offered the 'solution' of accepting our own inferiority and of seeking support from a member of the superior sex who can appear as our salvation.

Currently, women have no education of our own. There is only education designed by men, for men, in which we are permitted to participate — in men's interest.

Making women wrong

When Simone de Beauvoir (1972) tried to describe how the world looked from the subordinate position of women, she focused on the way women are always in the wrong. If, in the middle of a discussion, she said, a man says to me 'Oh you only think that because you are a woman', there is very little that can be done. It is not possible to reply 'And you only think your way because you are a man' because *woman* and *man* are not terms of equal value. In male dominated societies, she says, where men are more important – on the grounds that they are more representative, more authoritative – 'it is understood that the fact of being a man is no peculiarity. *A man is in the right being a man; it is the woman who is in the wrong.*' (1972; p15; my emphasis).

That men are in the right — by virtue of their sex and not because of what they say — and that women are in the wrong, regardless of what they say, is a fundamental principle in structuring and organising our society and it is a principle taught every day within the parameters of education. For women to have equal rights to find that men have decreed that women are wrong, is no right at all: indeed, it is playing into the hands of male control for women to demand more opportunities to be drilled in this particular lesson of their own inadequacy and lack of authority. The more proficient we become at our lessons, the less likely we are to challenge male dominance.

For centuries feminists have perceived this principle operating in the ordering of our society, and contemporary feminists have used the term 'male-as-norm' to represent this phenomenon. Feminists have recognised that this is a concept which has originated with men, but which women have been obliged to learn, in order to become members of society and to share the cultural, man-made view. The idea that the male is the normal, the representative, the paradigmatic human being, has its roots in male experience, and while men are in control, the objects and events of the world are judged against the male standard.

Whenever those who are not male reveal themselves to be different, to have different experiences and explanations, then rather than being seen as an autonomous but different group, their differences are seen as deficiencies. If the male is the norm, then those who are not male are deviants; while men see themselves as right, then any differences displayed by women can be seen as wrong; and men have the power to impose their value system on those who are not men.

The way that this principle of male-as-norm works can be illustrated by reference to almost any branch of knowledge from anthropology to biology and from psychology to history (see for example Dale Spender, *Men's Studies Modified: the impact of feminism on the academic disciplines*, where across fifteen disciplines it has been revealed that women are in the wrong, while knowledge is encoded by men).

For example one might suspect that language and the study of language could be neutral activities, but it must be remembered that men have made up the language, decreed the conditions of its use and set the framework for its study in a male controlled society and at all of these levels there is evidence that men have set up the rules so that men are right and women are wrong (Spender, 1980). Men themselves, of course, have not been responsible for collecting and collating *this* damning evidence, for gathering it together and presenting it under one heading or as one discipline called 'patriarchy', which examines and analyses the means and methods of promoting male supremacy, by passing off distortions as 'truths'. On the contrary, by creating a category called *objectivity* and applying it to the knowledge which they have generated, men have helped to pre-empt the development of such a discipline which would address itself to the problems of men putting women in the wrong, by using themselves as the human yardstick: if the knowledge men have produced is *objective* and true there can be no special subject which is concerned with the distortions and half-truths embedded in their knowledge.

Because men have been in control of the language as well as the disciplines they do not even perceive the necessity of labelling this phenomenon of men-are-the-norm and women-are-the-deficient-human-beings. These concepts have been labelled by women who are interested in naming male power and they are still — partly because of the newness — fairly bulky and unrefined terms. Knowing oneself to be in the wrong, by definition, before one even begins to do anything, is a daily reality for many women, but because it does not impinge on the consciousness of many men, like so many other aspects of women's lives it goes unnamed, it is not 'real'.

In the process of naming the objects and events of the world, men have used themselves as the reference point, as the centre; they have labelled the world in the light of their experience and have checked with each other for verification and validation. With their basis of shared experience they have been able to assure themselves that they have covered all contingencies, that together they constitute the limits of experience and what they see and know about the world is all that there is to see and know. The world, and all that in it is, is defined in relation to themselves.

What happens then when those who are not male present different descriptions and explanations of the world? What has happened to women over the centuries when they have said they do not see or know the same things?

This is no hypothetical question — when we rediscover some of the women of the past we find how readily and conveniently they could be classified as 'wrong' by not meeting some of the 'standards' that men decreed for them. Not measuring up in terms of femininity has consistently been, and still is, one way of discrediting women and thereby justifying their omission from the record. 'Disgraceful', 'bawdy' and 'immodest' were the accusations made against Aphra Behn and because of this it was perfectly proper not to perform her work after she ceased to write. 'A hyena in petticoats', Walpole said of Mary Wollstonecraft, and in 1803 when Mary Hays wrote her six volumes of biographies on women, Mary Wollstonecraft was left out so as not to give offence. Right up to the present day, where women such as Germaine Greer, Robin Morgan, Mary Daly, and Adrienne Rich — all making a similar protest to those of Aphra Behn and Mary Wollstonecraft — are abused, ridiculed, and are said to be aggressive, shrill, humourless, vicious, and very, very wrong.

While men have a monopoly on defining the world they have the opportunity to define women who do not agree with them as wrong. They are in a position to dismiss alternatives women may generate, to deny names for the thoughts and experiences of women where they are different from those of men. Instead, like Rousseau, they can provide standards which serve the interests of men.

And the women who meet these standards? What of those who learn to accept, to defer, to become modest and agreeable? We are still 'wrong' because we demonstrate our 'inferiority' to men.

The standards, the meanings, the names that men have decreed for women, from aggressive to agreeable, may be most inappropriate for women, but they have been the only ones available. We may choose how we wish to be wrong, as feminine or unfeminine, but we have little or no choice about being, by definition, in the wrong.

When women attempt to describe and explain the world independently of the descriptions and explanations provided by men, one of the most central features is that of male dominance, but any account and analysis of this dominance is undoubtedly subversive and even threatening to those who are dominant. This is why many men, with their vested interest in male control, will go to considerable lengths to suppress the ideas. Sometimes, however, the suppression and censorship is not completely successful and some of the ideas of women do slip through (particularly when women practise 'deceit' and publish under male pseudonyms for example), with the result that such women have to be discredited. But this is not an insurmountable or even difficult problem where society has been led to believe that women are in the wrong.

Aphra Behn slipped through — how, it is not quite known, but while her plays were so enormously successful and the theatre owners made so much profit, they were prepared to let her continue.* But her literary colleagues expended much effort in proving that she was wrong. She was a woman.

She was abused and ridiculed, accused on the one hand of being *feminine*, and therefore unable to write (it was frequently suggested that a man, probably her lover, was writing her plays for her), and on the other hand of being unfeminine and therefore her plays were unacceptable. No matter what she did as a successful writer, challenging male supremacy, her male colleagues were able to argue, by the standards that they set, that she was wrong. Males today are still able to call on these same standards and behave in the same way to discredit women, as many women who have spoken out against male supremacy can testify.

No matter what grounds women may have for stating their own case, men can dismiss it as wrong, for women are wrong according to their schemata. Women's experience is not part of the accepted comprehensible social experience, which is male experience, so women who attempt to describe and explain the world from their perspective — which includes the experience of being wrong — can be readily dismissed while males are in charge of what we know and understand.

Every aspect of *their* male language serves to reinforce *their* male belief that women are in the wrong, and because *we* have to use their language *we* begin to acquire their beliefs. From birth we are bombarded with the belief that men are more important, and that we

*It is not uncommon to find that the profit motive overcomes other vested interests: it is one of the reasons why publishers publish feminist books today.

have less authority to think and act in the world, that we only exist in relation to them. When we look for contrary evidence not much is to be found — not because it has not been there, but because it has been removed. So we doubt. We doubt our own feelings and our ideas. We search for words which encode our meanings, which describe how we feel and think, but the words are not there. So we doubt more. Each day of our lives we are informed that women do not count, that we are wrong, that our different descriptions and explanations are ridiculous or unreal. If we try to insist on their validity, we can be discounted again, as aggressive or emotional (unfeminine *or* feminine, but either way *wrong*). With nothing to confirm our explanations of our own lives, we begin to deny our existence, to repudiate our explanations and our lives. We learn that we are wrong: we become educated.

In our daily lives men define the topics and provide the terms for describing and explaining the world, and we are silenced and interrupted as were our predecessors. We are given little space to forge our meanings and little or no opportunity to share them or pass them on. The issues we want to discuss and the way in which we want to talk about them can all be classified as wrong and dismissed. Even when we attempt to talk about the issues that men have named, but from our perspective, we are frequently treated as unreasonable or neurotic. If we want to discuss our experience of language where we are consistently silenced and interrupted we are usually dismissed because, after all, the reality decreed by men is that women are the talkative sex.

Our absence, invisibility, inadequacies, and deficiencies are massive in the knowledge encoded by men, the extent of our wrongness is overwhelming in the record of male knowledge into which we are initiated and in which we are required to be competent, even to excel, if we want to qualify as 'men of learning'.

If after all this there are some of us who persist in declaring that we are not wrong, except by the standards that men have evolved, if we insist that we, as women, as half the human population, shall decree our own standards for ourselves, and reject the standards imposed on us by men, then men can use another weapon they have constructed: they can declare that we are being subjective. Men's views are right because they are men: men's descriptions and explanations which arise from their experience of the world are legitimated by themselves as objective. But where women's expressions do not conform, where they arise from women's experience of the world, men are able to label the differences as subjective.

As Adrienne Rich (1979) has commented, objectivity is the name we give to male subjectivity, for most, if not all, of the knowledge that is readily available in our society, has its origin in a male version of experience and is therefore limited because it is based on nothing other than the subjectivity of men, who have been able to decree that what they do is right and what women do is wrong. This is how power breeds power, for those who are in power can set the terms and they can make those who are not in power, in the wrong.

Teachers can constantly cast students in the light of being in the wrong. Referees can do it to players, television interviewers can do it to interviewees, because all have the power to define the terms and to define their own position as 'right'. And students, sports people interviewees, and women can all be labelled as 'emotional' if they attempt to protest that the terms are not fair. If those without power were to have power, then they could (if it were desirable or necessary) reverse the whole process.

In 1980 I gave a talk at a conference on sexism and education, in which, as the speaker, I had the power to define the terms. I discussed the way in which in mixed-sex contexts men talked more and interrupted more. Some of the men were quite angry: they challenged what I was saying (and with the excessively long speeches and constant interruptions at the end of the lecture unwittingly substantiated my argument) and protested vehemently. Because I had the power to define the terms it was relatively easy to label their behaviour (according to the categories they had devised) as emotional and subjective.

I did not do this because I genuinely believed that their behaviour was emotional and subjective: on the contrary I think it logical, reasonable and predictable that those who do not define the terms and who are cast in the wrong should protest. I wanted these men to share some of the daily experience of women.

My efforts were not appreciated: the links were not made. Being perceived as the constant talkers and interrupters was not the experience of these men; being cast in the wrong was not a common or familiar state; protesting, and being labelled as emotional and subjective, heightened their sense of injustice rather than quietening them. Used to being in the right, they were affronted by my suggestions and increased their efforts to discredit me, and all the time they added to the evidence. Women began to laugh and the 'emotions' became more intense.

For these men I had set up a double-bind. In their minds they were damned if they accepted what I said (that they were unjust, unfair, talked more and interrupted more) and damned if they challenged (by talking more and interrupting more). Yet this is the double-bind that men have constantly set up for women who are wrong if they go along with male schemata (and conform to the model of femininity which is less prestigious than that of masculinity) and who are wrong if they do not (and act unfeminine).

In our society it is women who are wrong as a condition of existence while males are in control (and the occasional examples where women have a small measure of power for a short period of time do little to dislodge this overall belief even if they can help illustrate the mechanisms by which it is maintained). Virtually every aspect of our education, everything we are taught by a patriarchal society, is based on the premise that women are wrong, and the more we are educated, the more we learn about our own ostensible deficiencies. We are initiated into the belief that the knowledge we generate as women is subjective, and subjectivity is something to be despised, condemned and avoided at all costs. In generating our knowledge we engage in precisely the same processes as men, but when we do it we are wrong.

Even if we do it 'better' as some researchers have indicated (such as Peter Trudgill who suggests that women talk 'better' and Kathy Clarricoates who has shown that girl students behave 'better') this serves as grounds for explaining why we are wrong. For men have developed a rationale to dismiss what we know as women — no matter what it is — and to elevate, enhance and enshrine what they know as men, no matter what it is. They are right, according to them: their knowledge is to be classifed as objective and rational and is to be praised and accepted, not just by them but by women as well.

This is the sexism women are up against in education. It is a system in which we are wrong: our lives are wrong, our knowledge is wrong; and only when we accept these tenets and deny our validity and autonomy, can we succeed in education. We have to *master* our lessons, to learn to do things the male way and the right way, to learn the value of objectivity — the male view, and to repudiate the value of subjectivity — the female view. We have to be able to construct knowledge in the same manner as men on the same topics as men, which means we have to make women invisible and keep them off the record, if we are to get our qualifications and succeed.

And if we do not reach these standards that men have laid down, we are once more 'wrong', we are said to underachieve.

We must learn the history of men, the literature of men, the language of men, and the sociology, psychology, anthropology, philosophy, biology and science of men, and in all of them the existence of women as an autonomous group and the validity of women's experience is denied, or dismissed as deviant. While it would seem plausible that we should know and appreciate the struggle and pain which accompanies domination and exploitation and that we should be able to describe and analyse the world and encode knowledge from this perspective which is shared by dominant and exploited groups the world over (which as Elizabeth Janeway, 1980, has emphasised, *all* include women) our understandings and insights are kept off the official records so that what is encoded and taught, what is the substance of learning, is the knowledge made by men and about men. Not only may we be informed that our perceptions are of little value, we may also be told that they impede and interfere with research; that 'subjectivity', often our experience of the world, is to be avoided because it distorts the results!

What we need to appreciate is that the problem of sexism and education will not be overcome by inserting some positive images of women in the curriculum, by appointing a few more women to senior posts or even by encouraging girls to stay on longer at school and reach the relatively higher standards of their brothers so that they no longer 'underachieve'. Such 'solutions' do not even begin to tackle the problem.

We cannot even argue that sexism should be removed from the curriculum for there would be little or nothing left of existing learning that could be taught. If we were to take out of education methods of constructing knowledge which cast women in the wrong, and findings which demonstrate that women are wrong, not only would material for the curriculum be very scarce, we would also have to examine different possible explanations for why the world is as it is: if women cannot *a priori* be blamed (as they have been from Eve onwards), where and how shall we begin to explain the world?

Sexism is no bias which can be eliminated but the foundation stone of learning and education in our male controlled society. It is one of the means whereby males have perpetuated male supremacy and control and we must explicitly acknowledge what it is that we are doing when we expose those practices and their purposes. What we are doing is challenging male control at a fundamental level. It is not a level which is challenged when we argue for more women writers in a literature course, for example, or for some 'women worthies' to rank alongside the 'male worthies' in a history course.

Over the last ten years women have been developing insights and understandings about the way in which men control knowledge and learning: we have articulated and developed some of the concepts which are consistent with our view of the world (concepts such as sexism, male-as-norm, patriarchy) and because we are now in a position to be able to identify some of the mechanisms of male control, we are also in a position to do something about it.

We do not have to accept that we are inadequate in some ways for the onus of explanation and justification has shifted. It is no longer that we are inferior (or unlearned) but that we know we have been systematically denied knowledge about women and about male dominance. We can ask why men have not permitted the free flow of knowledge and make it *their* responsibility to justify the omissions, and not, as has been the case in the past, *our* responsibility.

We can refuse to learn the lesson that we are wrong, and insist on our own right to set our own standards. We can describe and explain ourselves in a way that is consistent with our own experience instead of trying to conform to the pictures that men have created of us, in their own interest. We can argue that in the interests of arriving at more complex and comprehensive understandings about the world and human beings, our experience must become part of the record and must be valued.

Part of our experience is of male dominance and why and how men have labelled themselves as right and women as wrong, and what we must work to ensure is that these understandings do become part of the culture's understandings, and are transmitted to the next generation. The history of the women's movements is cyclical — there have been periods when women have generated as much knowledge about male control as we have today, if not more (see for example Elizabeth Sarah's forthcoming book, *A Cautionary Tale*), only to have that knowledge disappear in a very short space of time. Fifty years later women have to begin again without the benefit of building on what has gone before. We need to keep women *on the record*, to name the problems of the world from women's perspective, to belie the belief that women are wrong, and to develop a body of knowledge that focuses on dominance and oppression with all its ramifications. And we need to hand on what we know for, ironically, once our understandings are accepted and valued, they will also change. If and when the world is described and explained from the multiple perspective of human beings (and not just the dominant group), if and when knowledge is encoded by all, and forms part of the record for all, we will not be living in a patriarchal society as we know it today. We will not have a sexist system of education.

3 Setting Up the System

The system of education which is supposedly *our* system was set up by men long before women were permitted entry. It is important to note that many of the demands for female equality have been demands for equal access to the education which men have devised — which for many reasons is no equality at all. What constitutes education, what is believed to be worthwhile and necessary knowledge, what is accepted as a reasonable way of imparting knowledge, what is perceived to be a logical system of classifying and treating students, have all been formulated by men from their position of dominance and put into practice without reference to those areas of human experience which are the prerogative of women.

Educational equality for women will have been achieved when women's experience is accepted by society as equally valuable and valid as that of men, when half the knowledge that is available is generated by women and about women, when women are half the 'government of education', when women's ideas about education are equally viable and equally implemented with those of men. At the moment we are as far from achieving these goals as was Aphra Behn.

In England and Wales, Eileen Byrne (1978) has stated that 97% of the government of education is male, and this is no accident. Dorothy Smith (1978) writes 'Though women's participation in the educational process at all levels has increased in this century, this participation remains within marked boundaries. Among the most important of these boundaries, I would argue, is that which reserves to men control of the policy and decision-making apparatus of the educational system.' (p287). Men have decided what education will be and women who seek only equal entry to that system simply seek equal rights to the education of men which is designed to serve men. For women, equality will consist of equal *control* of education, and this is a very different matter indeed.

Because men got there first, they held all the powerful positions. They decided what would be taught, how it would be taught, and to whom it would be taught on the basis of the limited evidence that was available to them from their male experience. And while over the last centuries there have been some modifications in their ideas about who should be taught, and education was extended from the male upper and middle classes to encompass the working class, and blacks, and women of all classes and cultures*, there has been little or no reduction in the control of what will be taught, nor how it will be taught. Because of this, women's gains have been minimal.

Where some (few) women have entered the power structure they have been required to depend on male approval and support for their positions, and this has been one of the reasons that they have frequently 'toed the male line' rather than try to develop their own. Because of this, women, even in positions of power, 'do not ordinarily represent women's perspectives' explains Dorothy Smith (1978) for 'They are those who have been passed through this very rigorous filter. They are those whose work and style of work and conduct have met the approval of judges who are largely men. And in any case, they are very few.' (p289).

Men have set up the system and they control it. Such control can be used to appoint to their ranks only those who will help to *perpetuate* male control of *what* is taught and *how* it is taught. There is nothing so obvious as advertisements for candidates who profess staunch allegiance to the principle of male dominance, of course, but many means whereby 'the best candidates' for influential positions appear to be males, or females who are indebted to males.

The process pervades schools where, the further females and males proceed, the more they learn about men and their authority, and the less they learn about women, who are without authority. Most graduates of schools have been drilled in the differential value of the sexes, and both sexes can generally be relied upon to have learnt this particular lesson fairly well. The implications of this are significant, for without reference to individuals or to employment tasks, the general belief that males are automatically the *better candidates* has been fostered, so that there has been an accepted maxim that when all things are equal (as if they could be!), then it's better to choose a man.

Men have controlled not just education, but most social

---

*As mentioned in the introduction, most of the arguments in this book are equally applicable in terms of class or ethnicity where the knowledge generated by the working class or blacks has been disavowed and disallowed: the difference here is that I am generalising from the experience of women who comprise half of the working class and half of every ethnic community, whereas in patriarchal terms it is always the males of these classes or ethnic groups that receive attention, while the women remain invisible.

organisation as well, and there are other facets of the 'male as the better candidate'. With women organised to undertake childcare and home-making, for example, it is undeniable that many males are released from the responsibility of life-maintaining tasks and are more able to devote time and commitment to the job. They are also more mobile, being able to travel further to and from work since they are not required to deliver and call for children at the school gates, and also more mobile in terms of transferring from one district to another (for wives are expected to follow their husbands).

That there are probably one hundred good reasons for males being better candidates *vis à vis* females, however, says little about males and females, and a great deal about male control. There is no biological base for women being without authority, excluded from the curriculum, required to undertake the full responsibility of child-care (instead of half), of servicing children and another adult, and expected to follow men rather than to establish their own financial base. These are all social arrangements, which men have developed and which apparently are quite satisfactory for men. When women begin to look at these arbitrary arrangements (arbitrary in the sense that there are numerous possibilities) they do not appear satisfactory at all, and instead have overtones of a 'conspiracy' designed to keep women *unsuitable* as employees, in relation to men. Adrienne Rich (1980) has argued that *all* the social arrangements have been made by men to keep women dependent upon men, and this applies just as much to the system that men have set up in education, as to legal, political, and employment systems.

There are however women who fail to learn; women who remain unconvinced about the female lack of authority, who do not accept the justice of women's exclusion from the educational system (or for that matter the justice of any of the other social arrangements) and who will not subscribe to the principle that, when all things are equal between the sexes, then it is more reasonable to choose a man. They will not repudiate their experience as autonomous human beings and insist on the value and validity of their own lives. These are the women who cannot necessarily be relied upon to act in the male interest if appointed to influential jobs and it probably helps to explain why there are so few feminists in policy and decision making positions in Britain. Such women are *difficult*.

There are numerous ways in which they can be perceived as *unsuitable* for holding influential positions in the system men have set up: there are many areas in which they can be perceived as wrong, or deficient. For example, in a society which assumes the politeness and deference of women towards men as the norm (see Spender, 1980) women who do not defer to men are often judged by women and men as socially unacceptable. Women who try to assert the strength and independence of women (in a society in which men have not accorded women strength and independence) are bound to be labelled aggressive, which is not at all deferential, and there is no end to the number of jobs for which aggression in a female is disqualification. (Men, of course, who assert the strength and independence of men, are more likely to be seen as demonstrating firm convictions, as displaying qualities of leadership and decision making capacity. Such convictions — and the way they are evaluated — are not usually in conflict with those who are making the appointment.)

Again, we have come full circle, with the 'socially unacceptable' behaviour of some women — which helps to disqualify them from appointment to the system — telling us little about women and a lot about the system. But if women were ever in a position to devise their own system, and to define their own standards of social acceptability, for men as well as women, the current better candidates might find themselves in a rather awkward position of not being able to meet the required standard with their present attitudes and skills. Perhaps this is the reason that women are denied such power.

The ways in which men have set up the system so that women are disqualified as women are too many to enumerate but one of the most common justifications for keeping the ranks confined to men is that of arguing that women are not qualified. 'I'd simply love to be able to appoint a woman, if only there was one qualified' is the oft-reiterated explanation for an all-male board/committee/executive. If this were not such a serious issue it would have its humorous element as many men are able to deplore the success of their system.

While men are able to monopolise the influential positions, they can, of course, argue reasonably that women do *not* occupy these positions, and women, therefore, do not possess the qualifications or *experience*. That women do not have the experience of being in influential positions can and does become a reason for not appointing them to influential positions. This circular argument has a familiar ring: it is the one exposed by Aphra Behn over three hundred years ago, and a circular argument which has been regularly discredited. It is another version of depriving women of access to a particular area, or particular skills, and then blaming women for failing to participate or acquire the skills.

Theoretically, one might expect to find that such an argument did not make its presence felt within education and that it would be seen as logical to provide experience for the inexperienced, and qualifications for the unqualified. But that girls are *believed* to be poor performers at mathematics or science, or woodwork or football, is often the very reason given for not providing girls with mathematics or science or woodwork or football. Frequently deprived of the facilities which males have — for these activities which males are believed to be good at — the girls can emerge as poor performers in comparison with boys, precisely because the system has such results built into it: not because boys are better than girls, but because men set up the system.

Almost anywhere one cares to look in the present education system, one can find the superiority of the male being constructed and this is why it is crucial that women begin to demand to control their own education. Having only equal rights to help make male supremacy come true, is not having equal rights at all. It may not be necessary to set up two separate systems if it is possible for women to have equal rights in determining what happens in the existing system, but it must be noted that in a male dominated society, equality in terms of numbers is no guarantee of equality in terms of power — after all, women comprise slightly more than half the population. If the present values remained, in which males are considered 'better' because of their maleness, then even if half the policy makers were women, perhaps male authority could still prevail.

One of the reasons for suggesting this possibility arises from an appreciation of what can happen to women who may run the gauntlet and, despite all the obstacles, become members of the male circles and still retain their commitment to the autonomy of women. We can ask for example what happens to women in the government of education, those 3%, who may attempt to make decisions on the basis of their experience as women.

Again, we can find that such decisions, and the reasons for them, can all too readily be dismissed. Their views will necessarily be unorthodox if they see male control as a problem, and their different views can be perceived as incompetent views. Their actions are interpreted through the filter of women being in the wrong.

While the norm is that men are right, then an incompetent man is unrepresentative of his sex: while women are wrong, any perceived incompetence (which could mean difference) on the part of a woman is representative of her sex. Few would think it logical to say 'We had one male school principal, and he was awful: we don't want another' but 'We had a woman once and it didn't work' is not always decried as ludicrous.

Men have created the standards, the rules of sensible behaviour which govern our society, and they have done so in a way which flatters men, which permits preferential treatment for men, so that they emerge as the best candidates in the male controlled system. And male control extends to the justification for that system, for if women are not among the best candidates — so the argument goes — then it is women's fault. Many men can argue genuinely — from their position as men — that there is no prejudice, that there is no discrimination, that women have equal access to their system but choose not to take the right subjects, to obtain the necessary qualifications, to gain the right experience. If men perceive their standards, based on their experience, as the *only* standard (and the only human experience) then it is reasonable for them to argue that women simply do not 'measure up' in their terms.

However, their experience and standards constitute only *half* the human experience, and women's standards which have their origin in the 'underside', 'uncharted', subordinate and suppressed state of existence would be very different. But while men remain in control of education women will receive an education which helps to disqualify them from participating in the men's system.

While many people believe and assert that there have been real gains made by women in education over the last fifteen years, the statistics tell a different story, particularly in relation to the position of women teachers. Reorganisation in education appears to be accompanied by a reduction of women in senior positions. This happened in regard to comprehensive and co-educational schools, and was certainly appreciated in some quarters. As Jill Lavigueur (1980) has pointed out, R.R. Dale, the expert on co-education, envisaged comprehensives with headmasters, while women would take their (secondary) place as senior mistresses (p189). Perhaps his vision has been realised, for Eileen Byrne (1978) has said that 'the proportion of women in leadership roles has actually declined from 1965 to 1974 and provisional statistics since then suggest a continuing trend of decline.' (p219-220). There has been a persistent decline in the number of women holding headships and senior positions despite an overall increase in women staff.

This pattern in which more men and less women emerge in influential positions after reorganisation is not a feature of the past. When, in 1980, Adult Education Institutes in London are reorganised and suddenly there are two women principals, instead of

DES Statistics of Education 1965-1974. Teaching Staff

	Sex-balance Percentage			
	1965		1974	
Teachers	male %	female %	male %	female %
Primary				
All teachers	26.0	74.0	22.3	77.7
Headships	49.2	50.8	57.0	43.0
Deputy headships	37.4	62.6	40.0	60.0
Secondary				
All teachers	58.8	41.2	56.5	43.5
Headships	76.3	23.7	81.2	18.8
Deputy headships	60.0	40.0	65.0	35.0
Second master/ mistress	33.2	66.8	34.0	66.0

(Quoted in Eileen Byrne, 1978; p218)

seven, we have evidence that men are still ensuring that they emerge as the best candidates in their own system (Mary Hughes, 1981).

Now that men are entering infant teaching, we will soon find that men are becoming the heads of infant schools, despite their small proportion of the overall teaching population: they will be the best candidates. Men are disproportionately the heads of all schools and colleges even where men comprise a very small proportion of the staff. In a patriarchal society the rule is that the further up the hierarchy one goes, the more men and the fewer women are to be seen, because it is men who are the best candidates, so say the men at the very top.

There is of course nothing so blatant as the issuing of edicts or proclamations that men are right and men are best (one could almost wish that there were, for it would make discrimination so much more explicit); rather, every facet of the education system works harmoniously to project this picture so that it is accepted as the reality by all members of society.

At all the policy and decision making levels we find men making the policies and decisions in the interests of men and their reasons are backed up by the objective proof of researchers and knowledge makers. Discovering how men have set up this system is a fascinating exercise.

We have already seen how more knowledge is generated about

men, and more significance attached to male experience in educational circles, and this helps to support the present policies and practices of the education system. This could change if women were to have equal access to control because not only would we insist on the inclusion of *past* knowledge about women, we would also insist that more knowledge be generated in the *present* about women. We would insist that men cease passing off their knowledge about themselves as human knowledge and confine themselves to generalising about men.

For example, A. H. Halsey, A.F. Heath and J.M. Ridge recently published their authoritative treatise entitled *Origins and Destinations: family, class and education in modern Britain* and led people to believe that they were discussing *human* problems. They were not: their study was confined to males. If they included women they could not have reached the conclusions that they did (nor possibly confirmed their hypotheses, nor consolidated their 'reputations'). One of the reasons Halsey *et al.* were able to do their research and to pass it off as findings on the human and social condition was because it is men who approved and funded the research, and who control publication (see Spender, L., forthcoming).

If women had been in charge, things would have been very different. Tessa Blackstone (*THES*, 1980, January 18, p14) for example pointed to the inadequacies of their 'all-male-but-ostensibly-human' research and Sarah (sic) Delamont stated in a Letter to the Editor in *Network* (1981, January 19, p2) that not only do the authors confine themselves to males, they also impose their male bias on other studies which include both sexes: 'Halsey and his co-authors use "children" and "boys" interchangeably themselves' states Delamont, 'but this is hardly an excuse for such carelessness in quoting from other sources.'

Unlike Sara Delamont I would not call this practice 'carelessness'; it is not a mere mistake, a departure from normal procedure. On the contrary this is what men have been doing for centuries in the system they have set up to eliminate women from the record (see Spender, 1981, *Women of Ideas – and what men have done to them!*).

Can we send our students with confidence to such books as *Origins and Destinations* if they contain such careless mistakes, asks Sara Delamont, making the implicit assumption that there are other studies in which the male-as-norm bias does not operate? 'Surely we deserve better' she adds, and of course we do, but not just from Halsey & Co. We deserve better from *all* research, in *all* disciplines, but we are unlikely to get less sexist nonsense while knowledge remains under male control, for it is inherent in the male controlled system that males will assume that their experience is more significant, that they constitute the norm and that their assumption will not be fundamentally challenged while they check only with other men.

Their assumption is quickly challenged by women — Sandra Acker, Tessa Blackstone and Sara Delamont — and it is easy to see how things would be very different if women were in control and men were accountable to women for half the time. But while women are marginal in the system men have set up, even their criticisms can be trivialised and dismissed, as is evidenced by the defence offered by Halsey & Co. Women, they explained, were not included in their study because women not not included in previous studies (Blackstone, 1980; p14).

Such a defence is ludicrous. First of all they are mistaken, for women have been included in previous studies, but they have chosen to ignore them and to call them males in the continued attempt to make women invisible and to remove them from the record. And secondly, by their own reasoning Halsey *et al.* are arguing that women should be kept out of present and future studies precisely because men have kept them out of past studies. Aphra Behn would have been able to use her analysis to expose this absurdity as well.

While men remain in control there seems to be little likelihood that there will be modifications in the practice of denying the existence of women. The paltry excuses offered by Halsey *et al.* might be sufficient to dispel male doubts about their credibility, but would not satisfy women who are wise in the ways of being excluded. Even the chances of obtaining their initial funding would have been severely reduced if they had been applying to a female funding agency: had they argued that their research was on human beings (when it was only on males) the error of their ways would have been pointed out to them, and had they requested to undertake a survey on males only, their application might have been rejected, on the grounds that their study was too limited.

Perhaps they suspected that they would not have been able to obtain the same results if they had included women, and this might have jeopardised their findings and rendered their research a 'failure'. Knowing that women can 'interfere' with theories and results, some social scientists have explicitly excluded them as research subjects. In commenting on the origins and reasons for the introduction of women's studies, Sheila Tobias (1978) has said that new research on women had to be undertaken because in so many disciplines it was found 'that where females do not behave as expected in experiments meant to test psychological and sociological hypotheses, the female subjects are considered to have "skewed" the data, and are rejected as subjects,' but, she adds, 'the hypotheses about "human" behaviour, however, survive.' (p89). Lee Jenkins and Cheris Kramarae (1978, 1981) have also shown how theories are based on men, and when women perform differently, the women are seen as 'peculiar' rather than the theories based on males seen as limited.

In her research on education studies in Britain, Sandra Acker (1980) found that where the theories are based on men, and women reveal differences, researchers are more often puzzled or perplexed by these differences than they are eager to revise their theories so that women are taken into account. In the findings that she surveyed, Sandra Acker found that 'Witkin is puzzled "as the findings for girls in secondary modern schools were not anticipated". For Synge, the high educational aspirations of rural girls were "contrary to expectations". Robinson and Rackstraw admit "at present we have no supportable explanation to offer for these occasional sex differences in performance". Liversidge is surprised that working class girls' occupational aspirations don't differ much between those in grammar schools and in secondary modern schools, unlike those of boys. And Robertson and Kapur go so far as to say that their results for women students are bizarre.' (Acker, 1980; p9).

At this very moment there is a wealth of information being produced within education departments, which will be used by educational policy makers and administrators, as well as by training colleges, and which will influence what is taught and how it is taught throughout the education system; and that information contains the 'facts' that male experience is significant, predictable, reasonable, and to be valued, while female experience is irrelevant, unreliable, inexplicable and not data which need be taken into account. The system has been set up so that the reasons and justification for male supremacy are constantly provided and reinforced.

It is unlikely that these facts will be successfully challenged at the points where they are produced and presented, for these areas too are predominantly male controlled. It is mainly men who get the research money (for men are usually the best candidates with the best 'track records') and become the research directors, while women, where they are involved in the task, are generally the research assistants. If such women were to point out that the 'facts' are only those of male subjectivity, are limited, and therefore distorted and misleading, they would not always find that their protests are taken seriously (for examples, see Helen Roberts, *Doing Feminist Research*, 1981). As many women research assistants testified at the seminar *The Politics of Research*, held by The Women's Research and Resources Centre, even when they did register their objections, the male view, the male interpretation still prevailed, and they were frequently classified as difficult or incompetent and ran the risk of being unemployed in the future.*

Many women do not sit back and take all this. This is why there are alternative interpretations of the same data often put forward, why there are such books coming out as *Doing Feminist Research* and why there are such seminars and discussions of *The Politics of Research*. It is why many women are engaged in feminist research, and often unfunded feminist research outside institutions. But the knowledge which women produce, which is derived from women's experience and which takes male dominance into account, comes up against all the obstacles which have been discussed and more often than not is dismissed and denied, is prevented from becoming the understandings and insights of the whole society.

It has been extremely difficult for women to have their findings published (see Lynne Spender, *Unpublished Heritage: The Politics of Selection*, in press, for further examples) and yet, unless they are published, they cannot become known and form part of our cultural understandings. Over and over again the male controlled editorial boards, reviewers, advisers, choose not to publish the knowledge of women — partly because there are at least one hundred reasons in patriarchal terms for such knowledge being not the best available, not the most scholarly, not the most useful, reasonable, necessary or significant knowledge. When men's problems determine the parameters, women's problems are, at best, marginal.

Because it has been difficult — some would say impossible — for knowledge about women from the perspective of women to obtain publication, many feminist publishers, editors, *etc.*, have emerged over the last few years and knowledge about women *can* get a hearing but often only a very limited one. Because men control the channels through which knowledge enters the education system it is relatively easy for them to erect barriers and to prevent this knowledge from being accorded value and becoming part of educational theory and

* It is no accident that the position of research assistant is usually temporary and without security and this makes many women vulnerable for they are constantly seeking new jobs and require references from (male) research directors.

practice.

For example, one channel is the *British Research Index* which claims to 'list and analyse the subject content of all articles of permanent educational interest'. As no one could be expected to read all the latest research reports in Britain, the *British Research Index* has a staff which carries out this task, which makes a selection from all that has been published, and guides those who consult it towards the most important and significant work. But while 195 journals and publications are combed by the staff, none of the 195 is a feminist periodical (despite the fact that there are many in Britain and they have all covered aspects of education). Feminist material will have a difficult time entering the mainstream if it relies on this channel!

Not only is knowledge about women kept out by this process but because the *Index* serves as a guide to current issues, because it is supposed to be a record of current concerns and understandings, it also suggests to those who consult it that there is *no* feminist research being undertaken, that this is not an issue, that no one is engaged in work on the area. It is the same process which has kept women off the record for hundreds of years and just as we assume that we have no predecessors who have been concerned with the issues that claim us today, so will future generations of women be convinced that we did not exist — particularly if they look up the objective and prestigious Index.*

Again, it must be understood that the selection made by the *British Research Index* could be justified on the basis of standards — male standards. In terms of these standards it could be argued that knowledge about women is *not* of permanent educational interest — to men. This would not be partiality or bias, but reasonable and logical when only the subjectivity of men is what counts.

Throughout the entire education system at every point of power men are in control either in their own right, or through the appointment of women of whom they approve and who, because they are dependent on that male approval, can work to maintain male control. Men have set up the system so that it teaches the male experience of the world — and within that male experience men are far more important.

If women were to have equal access to control there would be enormous changes. Many of the best candidates according to men's

---

* The reality is of course very different. The research index at The Women's Research and Resources Centre contains literally hundreds of entries of research in progress on education. But the *British Research Index* does not seek this evidence. See Chapter 12 on Women's Education.

standards could quickly find themselves the worst candidates according to women's standards, if they could not recognise the limited and partial nature of male experience and modify their behaviour accordingly. Much of the current research would not get funded, many of the current findings would not be acceptable, some of the books and articles would not be considered sound and would not be published if women were making some of the decisions. The *British Research Index* and other comparable publications which purport to tell the whole truth while only telling half, would be called to account if they were accountable to women. The channels for insights, understandings, theories, to flow into mainstream education would not be blocked to women if women were equally represented among those who controlled them, if women were not dependent on male approval for their positions, but were able to act in their own right and in their own interest.

But this is a future goal and not a present reality. At the moment it is possible to produce reams of statistics which document the extent of male control (although, understandably, it is women who in the main collect them and attempt to publicise them*). While men are in control, however, and set the standards, even these starkly revealing statistics can be readily 'rationalised' as an indication that women do not measure up to male standards: men can call on considerable evidence which they have constructed, to 'prove' that this is the case.

Women, however, can 'rationalise' very differently, because while male dominance is not often a problem to men and does not normally figure in their explanations, for women it is central. Women can 'prove' that men have set up the system so that they can provide the evidence that they are the best candidates for influential positions: women can 'prove' that men have set up the system so that the problems of men are the only ones that are of permanent educational interest or significance, so that women are made to 'disappear', are kept off the record, and are classified as wrong. While for men, every appointment of a man as head, as director, as warden, as official, may 'prove' men are the best candidates, for women this constitutes proof that men have set up the system so that it works in the interests of men!

*WEdG, the Women's Education Group, is currently compiling the statistics on ILEA because they know the authorities will be embarrassed at the stark exposé of where women are in the system.

Part Three
In the Classroom

4 Make Trouble – Get Results!

Historically, men have excluded women. They have proved that women are inferior and wrong and therefore do not deserve the same consideration and opportunities as men. Historically men have interrupted and silenced women and have catered for the interests of men. But anyone who assumed that this was only history would be being misled, for this same process continues today in most of the classrooms of this country, where, in mixed-sex classes, males are the authority figures, males do the talking, and lessons are designed to cater for male interests because, as most teachers acknowledge, if males do not get what they want, they are likely to make trouble. At this moment, female students are being dismissed in class in exactly the same way as their foremothers have been dismissed, and the experience of women is no more likely to be the substance of the curriculum in a mixed-sex school than the experience of women has been the substance of our social knowledge.

It is not difficult to establish who gets the teachers' attention in class, and numerous studies report that boys get most of it in mixed-sex classrooms (see Sears and Feldman, 1976, for an overview of this, and Birgit Brock-Utne, n.d.). But while it has been known for a long time that boys get so much more attention from teachers than do girls, not surprisingly, few attempts have been made to explain this phenomenon or to speculate on its significance: in a society where men are perceived as more important such statistics can simply serve to confirm what we already know about male 'supremacy' and are therefore taken for granted rather than made the subject of further enquiry.

Teachers themselves are very often unaware of the way they allocate their time and it is not uncommon to ask teachers whether they give more attention to one sex than the other, and to have them vehemently protest that they do *not* and that they treat both sexes equally. But when their next lesson is taped it is often found that over two thirds of their time was spent with the boys who comprised less than half of the class. Most teachers do not consciously want to discriminate against girls, they say they do want to treat the sexes fairly, but our society and education is so structured that 'equality' and 'fairness' mean that males get more attention (see Spender, 1981, a).

If the teachers do not know that they give more attention to boys, and more *positive* attention that enhances the image of boys, the students *do* know. In her recent study in Cambridge, Michelle Stanworth (1981) asked the students who it was who received the attention in class and what sort of attention they received and the students indicated that it was overwhelmingly boys who received the attention and who were given the knowledge that they were important and liked.

In classroom discussion, said the students, boys predominated: for every four boys who participated, there was only one girl. When teachers asked questions they asked two boys to every one girl, and when teachers provided praise and encouragement three boys received it to every one girl. And in these classes there were more girls than boys.

The students themselves provided the data that the boys asked twice as many questions as the girls and made twice as many demands of the teachers' time. And both the boys and the girls stated that teachers are more concerned about boys, they consider boys more conscientious and capable, they get on better with the boys, they enjoy teaching the boys more and are twice as likely to consider boys the model pupils (Stanworth, 1981).

Despite what teachers may think or say they are doing, from the perspective of female and male students there is consensus that boys are considered more important, more authoritative, more deserving and worthy of attention, and this knowledge possessed by the students adds to the confidence of the boys (who go on to say more and demand more attention) and undermines the confidence of the girls (who react by saying less and by attracting less attention). These are the lessons learnt in the classroom from kindergarten to college.

Teachers who teach the lesson that boys are more important than girls are not debased and cruel individuals who are deliberately trying to create or reproduce a sexist society: on the contrary many can be consciously trying to combat sexism. When I and many others have actively tried to change our patterns of behaviour in the classroom, when we have tried to change the proportion of time spent with the girls, the curriculum materials we use, the topics we set for discussion, we have often been spectacularly unsuccessful and for numerous reasons (see also Elizabeth Sarah, *Interaction in the Classroom*).

One reason is that sexism is so pervasive and embedded in our ways of looking at the world that we are sometimes unaware of the extent to which it controls our actions so that even when we feel that we are being just and fair, or even showing 'favouritism' to the girls, empirical evidence can indicate otherwise. Because we take it so much for granted that boys are more important and deserve more of our time and attention, giving the girls 35% of our time can feel as if we are being unfair to the boys.

While it is 'normal' to devote most of our efforts to boys, then even giving slightly more than one third of our attention to the girls seems to be a significant intervention and feels like making an effort to achieve equality.

I have taped many lessons that I and other teachers of mixed-sex classes have taught and there have been numerous occasions when the explicit aim has been to spend an equal amount of time with both sexes. At the end of the lesson I have felt that I managed to achieve that goal — sometimes I have even thought I have gone too far and have spent *more* time with the girls than the boys. But the tapes have proved otherwise. Out of ten taped lessons (in secondary school and college) the maximum time I spent interacting with girls was 42% and on average 38%, and the minimum time with boys 58%. It is nothing short of a substantial shock to appreciate the discrepancy between what I *thought* I was doing and what I actually *was* doing.

Other teachers have also been reasonably confident that they have achieved their aim of allocating their time equally between the sexes only to find when the tapes have been analysed, that spending approximately 38% of their time with girls feels like *compensating* the girls, feels like artifically constructed equality.

'I was so conscious of trying to spend more time with the girls that I really thought I had overdone it' one teacher said in amazement when she listened to the evidence of the tape and worked out that in her interaction with the students only 36% of her time had been spent with girls. 'But I thought I spent more time with the girls' said another who found that she had given them 34% of her attention, 'and', she added 'the boys thought so too. They were complaining about me talking to the girls all the time.'

It should not be surprising that the students should share a similar notion of fairness with their teachers, for we are all members of the same society which accords more significance to males. In the classrooms where teachers were trying to allocate their time equally, their efforts did not go unnoticed by the students, and despite the fact that the teachers were unsuccessful, and were able to spend only slightly more than one third of their time with the girls, many of the boys protested that slightly more than one third was unfair, and that they were missing out on their *rightful* share of teacher attention.

'She always asks the girls all the questions' said one boy in a classroom where 34% of the teacher's time had been allocated to girls. 'She doesn't like boys and just listens to the girls' said another boy where boys had interacted with the teacher for 63% of the time; and these are among some of the more 'polite' protests. From this it would seem that in a sexist society boys assume that two thirds of the teacher's attention constitutes a fair deal and if this ratio is altered so that they receive less than two thirds of the teachers' attention they feel they are being discriminated against.

Many exercised pressure on their teachers in the classroom but some even went further and either complained, or threatened to complain, to those in authority, about the preferential treatment girls were receiving when allocated more than one third of the teachers' time. And this is another reason that teachers are unable to give an equal allocation of time to the sexes — many of the boys are against it, they make trouble and they get results.

Every teacher must try to gain the interest and co-operation of the class. There is only one teacher and many students, and if there is to be 'order' as it is generally understood, then teachers are usually in the position of trying to utilise the interest and goodwill of those whom they are required to teach. In today's classrooms, the point of view of students is often taken into account — in some areas — far more than is generally acknowledged and it makes common sense to many teachers to enlist the co-operation of their students.

But many males will co-operate only when it is their interests that are taken into account. This means that teachers are not always free to introduce either the forms of discussion or materials they would like. Rather than catering for the class as a whole, in mixed-sex classrooms they may find that they are being manipulated by a group of boys who will engage in uncooperative and disruptive behaviour if they do not get material they find interesting.

This raises the question of what is interesting in general in our society. It has already been established that knowledge about women is not valued — is not considered interesting or significant except by a few funny feminists — and therefore, even if knowledge about women were readily available it would not serve the purpose of claiming the attention or the respect of some boys. On the contrary, introducing knowledge about women (and trying to spend more time in interaction with female students) is more likely to result in a riot than in reasoning.

What is considered inherently interesting is knowledge about men. Because men control the records, and the value system, it is generally believed that it is men who have done all the exciting things: it is men who have made history, made discoveries, made inventions and performed feats of skill and courage — according to men. These are the important activities and only men have engaged in them, so we are led to believe. And so it is that the activities of men become the curriculum.

Making male knowledge the substance of the curriculum is a multifaceted process. A part is played by those who determine what the values of society will be, a part is played by the policy makers and a part is played by the researchers who produce knowledge about men; but a part is also played by male students in mixed-sex classrooms who insist that their interests be catered for — often exclusively. Many teachers can document what happens in a mixed-sex classroom where boys are not the focus of attention — there is trouble!

If boys do not get what they want then many of them are likely to be uncooperative and in a sexist society their lack of co-operation is often expressed in sexist ways. In a society where males are expected to be aggressive, to be authoritative, forceful and masterful, then in many respects boys are only doing what is expected of them if they act in an aggressive manner when registering their protests. Many teachers and students see it as quite legitimate for boys to make trouble, to prevent others from participating, to impose their values on others who may not share them, if they do not get what they want.

'The boys get upset if we try to talk about girls' things' said one female student, 'I suppose it's only right really.' When I asked her whether the girls got upset about having to do only boys' things she said, 'It's not the same. We don't mind doing their things. Sometimes we get upset but we don't say much.' When girls are required to do 'boys' things' they don't make as much noise, they don't mount the same disruptive protests. Girls do not impose their values on the boys, nor do they manipulate the teachers in this way.

Because teaching is so closely allied with classroom control in our society (an arrangement which might be altered if women were to have a say) teachers simply cannot afford to have a classroom of unruly boys who are not interested in the lesson and who are bent on causing trouble. The boys get the results — the lessons are directed towards them!

When Katherine Clarricoates (1978) interviewed primary

teachers they provided clear evidence that they geared their classes to the interests of boys (despite the fact that they also claimed they treated the sexes equally) because that was the only way the class could be controlled.

'Boys are more difficult to control' said one teacher. 'Yes' said another 'they're ever so lively and boisterous.'

'It's important to keep their attention . . . otherwise they play you up something awful.'

'The boys are more difficult to settle down to their work . . . they don't seem to have the same self discipline as the girls do, so its important to direct the subject at them.'

'I'd tend to try and make the topic as interesting as possible so that the boys won't lose their concentration and start fidgeting . . . '

'It's a bit harder to keep the boys' attention during a lesson . . . at least that's what I've found so I gear the subject to them more than I do the girls who are good at paying attention in class'. (Clarricoates, 1978; pp356-357).

This is part of the significance of teacher attention being directed to boys. This is why teachers give them more attention and offer them more praise and encouragement, and why boys talk more, make more demands, question and challenge more. This is the process whereby the *male* experience becomes the *classroom* experience, whereby education duplicates the patterns of the wider society.

For girls who are expected to be dependent and docile, any objections they may have to being inculcated in the male experience can take a different form. Their failure to co-operate can lead to withdrawal, to either 'getting on with the work' and not expecting it to be meaningful or interesting, or to quietly opting out in the corner. Either way, such behaviour of the girls is not likely to be seen as evidence that teachers cannot control their classes, for in most classrooms it is the noise level which is used as the criterion for teacher efficiency, and inside and outside education it is the male who makes the more noise.

The students know that girls are expected to be quiet and docile (and this has numerous consequences) and when Angele Parker (1973) questioned students, both sexes stated that asking questions, challenging the authority of teachers, demanding reasons and explanations — in short behaving in an active way in the classroom

— was a masculine activity. And both sexes know that girls who do not conform to these expectations are likely to be punished.

Over and over again my own research has exposed the double standard which operates in the classroom. When boys ask questions, protest, or challenge the teacher (or other students) they are often met with respect and rewards; when girls engage in exactly the same behaviour they are often met with punishment and rebuke. For boys who demand attention and explanations there is *not even a term in the language* to label their undesirable behaviour, but there is for girls — they are unladylike! It is expected that boys should stand up for themselves, that they should assert themselves, and even if and when this may be inconvenient for a teacher, it is behaviour from boys that is still likely to be viewed positively. After all, boys will be boys!

It is not expected that girls should act in an independent manner, and if they do, their behaviour is frequently seen as inappropriate, is viewed negatively, and in many cases is classified as 'a problem'.

Teachers can continue to treat their students in this sexually differentiated way and at the same time report their behaviour as fair and just, precisely because in our society males are perceived as more important. It feels fair and just to pay more attention to males, to accord more significance to their behaviour and more legitimacy to their demands. In a society where it is normal for males to receive preferential treatment, it is also normal to provide such preferential treatment in school.

The consequences for girls are many and varied, and none of them is good. It must be remembered that in the past decade an enormous amount of research has been undertaken which establishes the primary importance of learners being able to talk about their own experience as a starting point for learning. Yet we have an education system where not only is it extremely difficult for half the population to find an opportunity to talk — particularly to the teacher — but where the experience about which they could talk is seen as inappropriate, as not sufficiently 'interesting' to be talked about. (Needless to say in the research on using one's own experience as a starting point for learning, the influential work of such people as Douglas Barnes, James Britton and Harold Rosen makes no reference to the restrictions placed on females.)

If talking about one's own experience is essential to learning then it must be stated that girls have very reduced opportunities in mixed-sex classrooms — both because of the restrictions placed on their talk and the restrictions placed on their experience.

There can be no doubt that education helps to undermine the self-confidence and lower the self-esteem of girls (this is discussed more fully in following chapters) for they are surrounded by evidence that they are not as important as boys, while teachers give more time, attention and praise to boys, and the lessons they are required to learn present the experience of boys in a positive light. Girls have little choice but to accept what they are daily taught, that they are inferior and wrong.

Bowing to the wishes of the boys in their classrooms, teachers find that there is no shortage of material which is designed to cater for boys: most textbooks assume that the average human being is male, that male experience is the sum total of human experience, and that the activities of males are inherently more interesting and significant. Rather than challenging some of the sexist beliefs of society, many if not most textbooks serve to reinforce sexual inequality. Marion Scott (1980) surveyed *all* the texts used in one London comprehensive school and in her article 'Teach Her A Lesson' reports that sexism is rampant, for not only do the majority of textbooks enhance the image of men at the expense of women, they frequently present a distorted representation of the world which is even more sexist than the real world (pp114-115)*. This has to be seen as quite an accomplishment.

But what is learned in the classroom is not confined to the material presented in textbooks. Many insights and understandings can be forged within the classroom which do not depend on received knowledge. First of all, students can find out things for themselves — they can ask questions, make new connections, describe and explain the world in new and different ways; and if girl students were free to make such explorations, to articulate and validate their own experience, then the fact that most encoded knowledge was sexist would not be nearly so significant. They would have another avenue open to them, another possibility for expressing and valuing their own opinions and their own existence.

But such a possibility is usually blocked: the dynamics of the classroom are such that it is males who are in control and the opportunity to make their own knowledge about themselves rarely exists for girls. Instead they are constantly subjected to the lesson that they do not count.

The lesson takes many forms. Sometimes it is an indirect lesson taught by lack of teacher attention and interest. In the classrooms

---

* The extent to which textbooks show a more sexist view of the world than is experienced in the daily life of students — and the reasons for this — are discussed in Spender (1980) 'Education or Indoctrination?'

where I have kept a record, not only do girls get less teacher attention, they are required to wait longer for it. When boys seek attention, 'demand' is an appropriate word, and unless the attention is immediately forthcoming they can often make life very difficult for the teacher (and other students). But girls can be 'fobbed off'; their hands can be held up for ages and their often polite requests for assistance can go unheeded as the teacher is obliged to remain with the boys.

In general, boys take up more space, even when they are a minority. They take up more space on their chairs (legs frequently extended as obstacles to unwary travellers), their chairs and desks take up more space, they move around the room more. (They also frequently have more space outside the classroom in corridors and, of course, in terms of sporting facilities: it is not unusual to find large areas of school playgrounds reserved specifically for boys and if there is a division of the playground it is sure to be the girls who get the smaller allocation. This too can be seen as 'fair' in the same way that a smaller allocation of teacher time can be seen as fair.)

Some of these lessons which girls learn about their relative importance (or more precisely, unimportance) are not within the direct control of the teacher, for just as students are required to respond in some measure to the teacher, so too are teachers required to respond — in some measure — to their pupils. And they are required to respond more to males. This raises the question of whether girls should begin to act in the same aggressive and demanding way as many boys do, and apart from the fact that I fear for teachers if such behaviour were encouraged, I have other reasons for seeking different solutions.

First of all I don't think that such male behaviour is admirable and I see no reason to emulate it. While logically it is perfectly proper to suggest that it would be more productive if boys were to emulate the behaviour of girls, this suggestion rarely arises in a society where male behaviour is assumed to be the best behaviour. But secondly, it is in some ways 'artificial' to suggest to girls that they should act in an autonomous, effective and legitimate manner when every other piece of evidence they gain from the society around them suggests that they are not autonomous, that they are ineffectual and illegitimate. Such behaviour in the classroom would be a departure from the norm, an aberration if it were without social sanction, and could well lead to strengthened feelings of inferiority if it were to fail. And I think it possible that such attempts would fail.

This is because boys can not only make trouble for the teachers —

and get results — they can also make trouble for girls. They can use the evidence readily supplied by society that girls are inferior and debased, and they can use it against the girls *with* social sanction.

John Eliot (1974) found himself puzzled by the fact that girls did not participate in his classroom in the same way as boys; they did not ask questions, volunteer information or even discuss the topic at any length. While the significance of the choice of topic seems to pose no problem for Eliot — it was *War* — he nevertheless kept records of what happened in his classroom and found that even when a girl did try to speak, the boys were quick to interrupt, ridicule her, and silence her.

It does not have to be the teacher who establishes the rules and imposes the penalties, who permits boys to talk more, and talk more freely. It is often the boys themselves who lay down the rules and ensure that they are understood and adhered to by the girls: it is often the boys who hand out the penalties, and police the rules, as they do in mixed-sex conversations outside the school (see Spender, *Man Made Language;* 1980).

That boys do not like girls, that they find them inferior and unworthy — and even despicable — is a conclusion hard to avoid when observing and documenting the behaviour of boys towards girls in schools. In the tapes that I have made in the classroom there is the evidence that boys frequently make insulting and abusive (often sexually abusive) comments to girls. There is also evidence that more often than not teachers do not take them to task for this behaviour.

More often than not such attacks are ignored, rendered invisible by the teacher who does not notice (or pretends not to notice) such outbursts. Rarely, it seems, do teachers seek to make an issue out of such behaviour, and when I have asked why it is that such abuse is allowed to persist, even to go unchecked, the response has usually been in the form of an excuse: 'All boys behave like that at their age, it's a stage they go through' and 'It's best not to draw attention to it, they grow out of it you know.' Apart from the fact that I have grave concerns over what they 'grow in to', I cannot fail to notice that such an evaluation takes only the boys into account. What is the effect on girls of this vilification?

Most teachers, most boys — and even most girls — will, it seems, acknowledge that boys do not like girls and that this is normal and to be expected. If at times the boys exceed the bounds of 'decency' then it is probably better to turn a blind eye. What is present, but remains unstated, in this rationale, is that it is understandable that boys should dislike girls and that this should be expressed in terms of sexual abuse. The 'problem' is sometimes that boys go too far, not that there is something wrong with their sentiments.

Where this form of behaviour has been documented in the work place it has been called *sexual harassment* (Lin Farley, 1978; Catherine MacKinnon, 1979; Anne Whitbread, 1980) and it has been analysed as male behaviour, designed to intimidate women and to reinforce their inferior status. It is endemic in mixed-sex schools, and applies to females as a group and not as individuals. Initially I thought perhaps girls who challenged male authority in the classroom were likely to be the targets for male contempt, but while it is possible that such girls are the objects of more explicit abuse (which of course discourages them from attempting further challenges to male authority), male contempt is by no means confined to them but is far more generalised. Girls who are quiet, who accept male dictates in the classroom, are just as likely to be viewed contemptuously. Once more we see another example of girls being viewed unfavourably no matter what they do. The value judgement is attached to their sex rather than their behaviour, with girls who act in unfeminine ways being ridiculed and abused and girls who act in feminine ways receiving the same treatment. And girls are intimidated by this behaviour: it is another example of boys making trouble, and getting results.

Michelle Stanworth (1981) asked the students she interviewed 'Who would you least wish to be like?' and with the exception of one girl, they all named a girl. The reasons were various.

Interviewer: Who would you least wish to be like?
Male Pupil: I don't know, let's see (sorting through cards with names of classmates) Oh, one of the faceless bunch I suppose. They seem so anonymous. Probably one of the gaggling girls, let's pick one. Linda, she's ugly. Yes Linda.
Interviewer: Is that because she's ugly?
Pupil: No, but she seems to be immature, she doesn't contribute much to the class. She stands for everything I dislike.
(Stanworth, 1981; p43).

Girls are disliked by boys (and girls) for being non-entities, for being colourless, passive and docile, but they are equally disliked for being individuals and claiming attention, for 'speaking out too aggressively' and 'hogging the limelight'.

It is no accident of course that girls cannot draw on a body of knowledge about women to illustrate how inaccurate and partial are the beliefs about the unworthiness of the female. It is no accident that they cannot present evidence to counter the belief that women deserve contempt because they are women. Such evidence, while it may have been produced by women for centuries, is not handed on by men.

Without this evidence it is difficult for girls to challenge male control in the mixed-sex classroom. What arguments are they supposed to offer the boys who dismiss 'girls' things' as silly, who demand priority for their sex, and who cause trouble if it is not forthcoming? What arguments are girls supposed to use to validate their own experience when the ridicule of the boys draws on the basic social assumption that girls are unworthy and contemptible?

In the past men have excluded women from interaction, defined them as inferior, and blamed women for the lowly place they occupy, but this form of behaviour is not just characteristic of the past for it is acted out in classrooms everyday. Whether the lesson is history, English, science or mathematics (sometimes more especially so when it is science or mathematics), girls are being informed that they are not valuable, they do not count, their experience (which includes the experience of being subjected to male control by the male students) is not important or significant.

Many retreat. Overwhelmed by the evidence from the curriculum, the teachers and the boys, girls can accept their 'inferiority' and assume their 'proper' place.

Terrible as it may appear this does not mean that I see the case as hopeless and feel that nothing can be done to dislodge the beliefs and break the pervasive patterns. Women can develop their own ways without imitating the behaviour of men, and some teachers are already making subtle and significant changes (see for example Irene Payne's work in *Learning to Lose*, p174).

One of the reasons that male control continues in mixed-sex classrooms is because its operation has not been exposed. Instead of waiting for the repercussions that are bound to result from trying to allocate more time to the girls, it can be profitable to set for the class the task of determining who gets the teacher's attention. Not only does this help to pre-empt the complaint of unfairness when boys receive less than two thirds of the time, it starts to provide girls with the evidence that they need and which they can use.

One strategy which could help to overcome some of the present problems lies in women generating knowledge from the perspective of women which serves as an alternative and counters many of the myths made by men. Fundamental to the knowledge women generate is the problem of male dominance.

Even raising the question— *who talks most* — a question understandably not raised by men, pays dividends for women. Who takes up time, and space, who sets the topics for classroom discussion, who makes trouble when they don't get what they want? All of these questions can be answered within the classroom by the students themselves and all of them serve to generate knowledge and evidence about women's view of the world.

If space for single-sex discussion can be made available, so much the better for the girls, who, without having to defend themselves to a hostile audience, can explore and express their own experience in a male dominated society.

Currently men hold power and it is therefore not surprising that women should seek approval and confirmation from males. Girls who defer to male authority in mixed-sex classrooms are behaving in a reasonable and logical manner while they believe that such authority is justified. But once women begin to ask questions, male authority becomes problematic. Girls quickly perceive that it is unfair that boys should dominate classroom interaction, that they should determine the dynamics of the classroom, and by challenging the structures of the classroom they are removing many of the means by which male authority is constructed. The floodgates are open. There is not the same need to defer to males, not the same necessity to depend on males for approval.

It was once stated in a volume signed by John Stuart Mill — but on his own admission the ideas within it were generated by Harriet Taylor* — that it was not enough for women to be slaves, they must be willing slaves. When women begin to generate their own knowledge they are often no longer willing. Girls are no longer willing to think it fair that boys should have more of the teachers' attention, that girls should have to wait, that the curriculum should be geared to boys. The hold that men have over women may be pervasive but it is fragile, for it relies so heavily on women's consensus.

Within every classroom there exists the opportunity for making knowledge, even for using this new knowledge as a means of examining that which has already been encoded. At the moment these opportunities are geared towards the interests of males, partly because many males feel they have a right to such opportunities: but they can be used by women.

* See Alice Rossi, 1970, *John Stuart Mill and Harriet Taylor Mill: Essays on Sex Equality.*

5 Teacher's Pet

Despite the fact that boys may be more troublesome in class, that they may present difficulties for teachers and even circumscribe the options that are open to teachers in the classroom, it seems that most teachers (feminists are among those who have to be excluded) prefer to teach boys and that the students of both sexes know this. In mixed-sex classrooms most teachers know more about boys, they derive more enjoyment from teaching boys, they like boys more and they think boys are better students — and this encompasses students from primary schools to further education, and there are few grounds for suspecting that higher education would be remarkably different.

From the sample of teachers that Michelle Stanworth interviewed it is clear that teachers of both sexes knew more about the boys. To most of them the boys were individuals — they knew their names and they learnt them earlier, they could discuss their characteristics and idiosyncrasies. In contrast, whenever they had difficulty naming or placing a student, it was always a girl. One teacher listed the names of all the boys in his class and gave details of some of their interests and abilities and finished his discussion with — 'And the rest are girls'.

The girls were sometimes nothing but an undifferentiated mass at the periphery of the teacher's consciousness. Sometimes more was known about them but almost always teachers were unable to provide the same amount of information about girls as they could do for boys.

In Stanworth's sample another (male) teacher was asked what his first impressions were of Emma: 'Nothing really' he replied, 'I can only remember first impressions of a few who stood out right away. Adrian of course; and Philip; and David Levick; and Marion, too, because among the girls she was the earliest to say something in class. In fact, it was quite a time before I could tell some of the girls' apart.' When the teacher was asked who they were, he replied 'Well, Angie and her friends, Leonore and Helen. They seemed rather silent at first, and they were friends I think, but there was no way — that's how it seemed at the time — of telling one from the other. In fact they are very different in appearance' he went on to add 'I can see that now, one's fair and one's dark, for a start. But at the beginning they were just three quiet girls.' (Stanworth, 1981; p23).

Other teachers made similar comments: the girls did not make any impression on them, it took a long time to learn the names of the girls, it was easier to learn the names of boys, the girls merged into a mass and were difficult to tell apart, there was nothing distinctive about them. In short many of the girls the teachers taught were anonymous and unknown, they were faceless. And this is not just because they are quiet and reticent in the class for as Michelle Stanworth has pointed out 'the few male pupils who were reported by their teachers to be exceptionally quiet in class were, nevertheless, clearly remembered' (p24); the boys' quietness became part of their identity and individuality.

Greater significance is attached to the male and to male experience in our society and it is therefore reasonable to expect that this value judgement will make its presence felt in schools. In every facet of classroom life, from the curriculum to classroom interaction, it is demonstrable that more attention is paid to males with the result that teachers are more familiar with male experience and individual males. Teachers are behaving in a manner that is completely consistent with the values and beliefs of society when they favour males and this is probably one of the reasons that they perceive their behaviour as fair and non-discriminatory, even when empirical evidence can so readily reveal their bias.

But a crucial question arises — what are the consequences for girls of this favouritism? Both sexes are learning the daily lesson that teachers prefer to spend time with males, to discuss male experience and to know and understand the individual males in the class, and while one sex may thrive, may expand and develop as a result of this knowledge, the other sex surely will not. While the members of one sex are more likely to be treated as individuals, to have individual and idiosyncratic problems which require individual solutions, the members of the other sex are more likely to be seen as a group in which both the problems and the solutions are generalised.

No research studies have been undertaken on this topic: it is not a problem which presents itself to men, for while male students receive this preferential treatment the male educational experience is undoubtedly positive and all is going well. But in the absence of research it is not difficult to speculate on the significance of this differential treatment for the girls.

Being unknown and unnamed is often taken by students as a sign of rejection, it is evidence of 'non-existence' in the teacher's eyes; it is an absence of approval in a system which depends in large measure on the conferment of approval. For many girls, educational experience reinforces the message provided by society, that they are indeed invisible. And rejection and invisibility can be self-promoting and lead to increased feelings of rejection and invisibility as girl students 'withdraw', make fewer demands, and recede even further into the background.

In many classrooms, as teachers persistently spend more time with the boys, accord more value to male experience, treat the boys more as named individuals and identities, the pattern of making females marginal is relentlessly reinforced. The opportunities for breaking this pattern are very few.

Douglas Barnes (1976) has stated that teachers form opinions about their pupils as if they 'were quite unaffected by classroom events or by the teacher's own behaviour' (p163) so that the teachers may decide that the annonymous, undemanding girls are simply displaying their 'true characteristics' without ever suspecting or recognising that they, the teachers, have played a part in creating annoymous and undemanding girls. (It has been my experience that many teachers can be quite hostile to the suggestion that such forms of behaviour can be a reasonable response to teacher behaviour.) Having formed their ideas about their students, states Barnes, such assessments are 'then used as a basis for interpreting his (sic) future behaviour, and for justifying the teacher's treatment of him.' (p163). If teachers have decided that the girls in their classes are not as lively or as curious or as competent as the boys — and there are grounds for suspecting that many teachers make such assessments — then they are likely to give the girls, as a group, material which is considered appropriate for less lively, curious and competent students.

Nell Keddie (1975) for example has pointed out that students who are perceived as more capable are offered different tasks and activities, and are expected to behave in different ways, from students who are judged to be less capable. The result is that those who are perceived initially to have resources are assisted to acquire more, and those who are perceived to be 'deficient' in some way find that the reduced expectations that the teachers have of them can help to limit their own horizons, and to reduce the expectations they have of themselves. When these findings are applied to sex differences there are serious implications (as Alison Kelly, 1981, for example has shown in relation to science education) but they have not been systematically pursued. The frequent assumption is that the two sexes are provided with equal treatment and that the girls simply 'underachieve'. Girls, however, do not receive equal consideration — boys receive preferential treatment and this is reflected in their performance.

It is fundamental to any teacher training programme to stress the individual nature and needs of the student, and it is a maxim that teachers must get to know their students as individuals if they are to be effective teachers — and disciplinarians. But preliminary evidence points to the possibility that girls are not treated as individuals by teachers of mixed-sex classes. Many such teachers often know so little about the girls that they teach, that it is simply not possible for them either to plan or to provide individually appropriate material and responses. The girls are treated as a group — and as an inferior group — and the goals they are set and the feedback they receive is more likely to be consistent with their inferior and deficient status than with their individual needs. So the boys go on gaining resources and the girls go on being minimised. And if and when the girls make the rational response to this discriminatory treatment and do not perform as well as the boys — they are, predictably, blamed. It is their fault: they have underachieved.

I have witnessed this process at work in my own observations in secondary schools, where teachers of both sexes are more likely to treat the girls as a group but the boys as a collection of individuals whose particular differences must be taken into account (see Spender, 1978; p2). It is in my experience common practice, for example, for teachers to ask questions of individual boys whose names they know while addressing questions to girls as a whole (and questions which in themselves indicate reduced expectations, and which, of course, are asked much less frequently).

Teachers are more likely to position themselves closer to boys when asking questions, to draw on their knowledge of the personal details of boys' lives, and in many overt and covert ways to convey the message that boys are the preferred sex.

Male Teacher: Now James, did you get that work done? I was wondering about you, about whether you could manage question three . . . Derek, what about you, did you find it a bit tricky? . . . And Martin, I *bet* you did. No difficulties there, I expect. I was going to do some extra ones for you . . . What about you Simon? Any luck? Did you manage to get down to it or was the social life too much again? Too distracting, eh? . . . And how about the girls. Suppose you have all done it anyway.

In the interest of brevity I have removed the student response to these questions asked by the teacher, but four male students were addressed individually, even jocularly and affectionately. The teacher moved towards them, and even walked right up next to two of the boys. In contrast, the girls as a group were addressed from a distance and to my mind there was no 'warmth' in the routine question they were asked and almost a note of resignation about the non-event of the girls in the classroom. While the boys were invited to respond, even in a lively manner, the girls were not issued with such an invitation: no response was required of them at all.

The girls know they are not held in high regard. Many of them quoted examples of the way they were ignored or dismissed and some suggested that the only way to attract attention was as sexual objects: 'Oh Mr Smith, he notices Cynthia alright. He always sees her and asks her what she's been doing. He'll have a joke with her. But the rest of us aren't here as far as he's concerned. We don't turn him on!' (sixteen-year-old, London comprehensive).

The dismissal of females seemed to me to be even more pronounced in science and mathematics classes, and this was substantiated by the girls who, in the presence of male teachers only, felt as though they were devalued and dismissed. 'You know, I don't think Mr Lawrence has ever asked a single girl a question.' And: 'You wouldn't want to have your hand up to tell him there was a fire, if you were a girl. We'd all burn to death before he asked you what you wanted to say. The boys don't have to bother though, with their hands. He just talks to them all the time.' And another: 'It's like a comedy routine and the boys get all the parts. We never get into the act.'

Students use this information that their teachers provide to make judgements about themselves, and whereas boys more frequently receive positive feedback and make positive self-evaluations, girls are more likely to receive negative feedback (I am assuming that *no* feedback at all is also negative) and are more likely to arrive at negative self-images — which of course helps them to meet the demands of society, to take their 'proper' place in the world.

Said one female student to Michelle Stanworth, 'I think he thinks I'm pretty mediocre. *I* think I'm pretty mediocre. He never points me out of the group, or talks to me, or looks at me in particular when he's talking about things. I'm just a sort of wallpaper person.' (p33). And wallpaper persons do not bloom or flourish: they do not become intellectually curious or courageous. They wither away.

In another transcript, Michelle Stanworth documents another, not atypical response:

Interviewer: What is Mr Fletcher's opinion of you, as far as you can tell?

Female Pupil: I don't know, because my opinion of him changed quite a lot over the year. At first I thought he was quite good, quite friendly . . . Then I really noticed that he had some favourites, and he kind of despised, which is what I feel he does, some of the people.

Interviewer: Who does he despise, do you think, in this group?

Pupil: Well, there's some girls at the back who don't say anything, or don't talk, and he doesn't seem to encourage any of them to say anything, he just ignores them.

Interviewer: And is it those girls that you think he despises? It's quite a strong word, isn't it?

Pupil: Yes, well perhaps not despise. Perhaps he just looks down on them a bit, I don't know. It's just the kind of feeling you get if you're in that class.

Interviewer: That he doesn't have much respect for them?

Pupil: Yes.

Interviewer: Would he be like that with anybody who was quiet do you think, or is it especially with girls?

Pupil: I don't know. It's probably because there are quite a few girls in our group, that it shows like that.

Interviewer: And who are his favourites then?

Pupil: Well there's a couple of boys who are quite sporty and he kind of jokes with them, and he lets them go off from class to play their rugby and various things like that. And there's two boys he seems to talk to quite often outside class, and things like that.(p34).

The girls know what is happening but there is no frame of reference which can help them to classify, interpret or explain this situation. Providing such a frame of reference is not so great a task. Once the problem is named and explained from women's perspective, all this data which is stored in our heads can so quickly and readily fall into place. As Jessie Bernard (1975) has stated there is a 'click' phenomenon when, for women, the world is suddenly reconceptualised and where women's experience is suddenly meaningful and real — and where the factor which has been left out, *male dominance,* begins to assume central importance for women in the description and analysis of their lives.

Meanwhile, boys go on being teachers' pets and go on reinforcing male dominance and control, and for want of an explanation that is socially validated and accepted girls go on being undermined and deprived of confidence and self-esteem. As Kathy Clarricoates (1978) has pointed out, the process starts with entry to school.

In the primary schools, Clarricoates found that teachers preferred to teach boys, thought boys were more fun, and perceived them as better students — even when they were not doing as well in class as the girls.

'On the whole you can generally say that the boys are far more capable of learning, more nicer to teach.

Although girls tend to be good at most things in the end you'll find its a boy who's going to be your most brilliant pupil. (Clarricoates, 1978; p358).'

These are among some of the statements teachers offered about their students (and they were teachers who claimed they did not treat boys and girls differently) and when expectation plays such a crucial role in the growth and development of students we can see that the sexes know they have very different expectations to fulfil. The boys are the favourites, much more is expected of them; and a great deal of what is learned in class is the justification for this sexually differentiated arrangement — although outside feminist classrooms this is not often made explicit.

'I like doing subjects like geography and I do find that this is the area where the lads do come out . . . you know . . . they have got the scientific facts, they've got some geographical facts whereas the girls tend to be a bit more woollier in most of the things.

The (girls) haven't got the imagination that most of the lads have got.

I find you can spark the boys a bit easier than you can the girls.

Boys seem to want more exciting projects to do than girls, whereas girls will fall in with most things.'
(Clarricoates, 1978; p357).

By believing that boys are brighter (regardless of the evidence), by believing they are more important, more worthwhile, more exciting, teachers play a considerable part in helping these beliefs 'to come true': the students begin to act in accordance with these beliefs and expectations, and begin to behave in the 'appropriate' ways.

The preferential treatment given to boys in mixed-sex classrooms pervades virtually every facet of classroom life, and provided with this overwhelming evidence of their own inferiority it is surprising that girls do as well as they do rather than that their performance should not — according to some measurements — be the same as that of the boys. What emerges from the observation of many classrooms is that even where girls do perform the same as or better than the boys, this evidence does not threaten the basic and deeply entrenched assumption of many teachers that boys are brighter and therefore should be treated differently.

Again, Douglas Barnes (1976) has said:

'Some teachers consistently accept behaviour from some children which would earn punishment for others. One child may find that he is expected to be ill behaved and stupid, and experience frequent reprimands; he may be told that his speech is incorrect, and find that what he has to say is misunderstood or ignored. Another may find that the teacher listens to him and credits him with good sense, attributes good intentions to him, and responds appropriately to what he says. If such differences exist in the treatment of pupils one would expect it over years of schooling to generate in pupils quite different attitudes to school learning and the part which each can play in it.' (pp164-165).

Half the school population however is female and some teachers frequently accept behaviour from one sex that would earn punishment for the other sex. One girl may find that she is expected to be invisible and dull and may experience teacher rejection and lack of attention, she may be told that her behaviour is silly* or find that she is misunderstood or ignored. A boy may find that the teacher listens to him and credits him with good sense, attributes good intentions to him and responds appropriately to what he says. And because of this differential treatment the girl and the boy behave and perform in different ways and have very different ideas about their value and place in the world. Only in a patriarchal society could girls be blamed for learning this lesson.

Elaine Showalter (1976) has commented on the consequences for

---

* Florence Howe (1976) has stated that the options for girls in mixed-sex classrooms are to be silly or silent.

girls of the preferential treatment of boys. The female student learns, she says, that it is the male opinion that is important, and that studying the curriculum materials is akin to 'studying a different culture to which she must bring the adaptability of the anthropologist.' (p319). Education provides women with a long apprenticeship in negative capability on self-image and self-confidence — the longer they continue, the more they learn about their own inadequacy. The masculine culture is so all-encompassing that it is virtually impossible for female students to defy the evidence and develop a positive identity. 'Women are estranged from their own experience and unable to perceive its shape and authenticity' she says, because it is not mirrored and given resonance in the materials or interaction in the classroom. 'Since they have no faith in the validity of their own perceptions, rarely seeing them confirmed ... or accepted ... can we wonder ... (if) ... women students are so often timid, cautious and insecure if we exhort them to "think for themselves"?' (pp319-320). Can we wonder if they begin to believe in their own anonymity?

Some may find the evidence offered in this chapter convincing and damning, and it is important to note that Kathy Clarricoates' work was published in 1978 and has not as yet made an impact on mainstream education. This is not because it could not infiltrate educational knowledge in the space of three years: no doubt if she had discovered that girls were interfering with or inhibiting the learning opportunities of boys it would be headline news in the educational world. Overnight it could become part of the valued knowledge that was transmitted in the classrooms to trainee and inservice teachers. But she is outlining the problems of girls from the perspective of women.

The evidence of this chapter could be dismissed on grounds that have already been documented — that the research is not *objective*, that it is soft data, and personal, and even that the women who have generated this knowledge have a vested interest in these particular findings. I cannot speak for Katherine Clarricoates or Michelle Stanworth who have spent long and arduous hours in gathering their data (mostly unfunded) but I do not think they would dispute that we do have a vested interest in these results. Where we would protest — and be extremely angry — would be if men did not admit that they have an enormous vested interest in the results that they have produced!

We would also fail to be intimidated by the accusation that our work is not objective: when men have produced so many distortions and half truths about men and women, in the name of objectivity, we feel quite strongly that we can be forgiven for wanting something better.

We fully appreciate that the findings we are putting forward are not those which have been traditionally accepted, and that we require people to take on something that by conventional definitions is unreal, and even absurd. But we have checked with each other and are prepared to validate and legitimate our findings from our perspective as women: we accept the credibility of what we have observed in primary schools, secondary schools, further education, and higher education, because it matches with our own experience: this is our version of our existence and we will not deny it. We are simply starting with a different experience of the world which produces different assumptions.

We also expect our work to be taken into account in education. We have documented the problem and we require a response from policy makers, teachers and students. We do not expect to remain invisible and unheard.

6 Girls – Being Negative for Boys

What emerges from a study of teachers and students is that there is general consensus that boys are brighter. Teachers of both sexes are inclined to believe that boys are brighter, boys are inclined to believe that boys are brighter, and girls are inclined to believe that boys are brighter — regardless of the performance of the boys in the classroom. There is no great puzzle about the origins of this belief, but there has been little documentation of the way it operates in the classroom, and traditionally little attention has been given to the consequences that this belief has for boys and for girls.

In her study of primary school children, Kathy Clarricoates quickly found that even when by all conventional standards the boys were not performing as well as the girls, their teachers invariably believed they were brighter than the girls. In many ways, this is just another version on the theme that even when girls are 'better' they are still *wrong*. That the boys might not be performing as well as the girls was even the reason put forward by many teachers for spending more time with the boys, and for gearing the lessons to the boys, who were seen to have more potential, but were in need of being 'drawn out'.

'Boys are interested in everything and are prepared to take things seriously' stated one teacher to Clarricoates, 'They tend to ask the deeper questions while girls tend to be more superficial about subjects: they ask the "right" questions simply because it is expected of them.' (Clarricoates, 1978; p358).

This is one of the ways that the achievement of girls is devalued in the classroom, and the belief in the superior *potential* of boys is able to persist. Says Clarricoates, 'The capacity of the girls to be better behaved, more conscientious, cleaner and neater in all aspects of work and conduct, and the expectations of teachers in regard to this, leads to the wholesale theft of true intellectual development in favour of boys.' (p358). When girls perform *well* it is often explained in terms of their conformity — they ask the right questions because it is expected of them, they follow the rules because they are passive and dependent, their work is neat and tidy and therefore not 'creative'.

When boys do *not* do well, this is often explained in terms of their independence and their free spirits' — their 'wrong' questions are an indication of their divergent thinking, their failure to follow the rules evidence of their intellectual non-conformity, their often untidy work a sign of their creativity. Clarricoates argues that regardless of the performance of girls their efforts are not seen as positively intelligent, whereas, regardless of the performance of boys their efforts are not seen as negatively intelligent.*

There are standard (as well as feminist) studies that support Clarricoates' thesis. For example, Philip Goldberg (1976) provided college students with a series of articles to evaluate, and the same article sometimes bore the name of a female author and sometimes the name of a male author. Whenever the students thought they were assessing the work of a man, they evaluated it as far more impressive than when they thought it was authored by a woman (whose efforts were labelled mediocre) even though it was the same article. This is only to be expected, though, in a society where it is assumed from the outset that men are more authoritative and women are deficient.

Goldberg, however, was surprised by his results because the students were all women. But it is not at all surprising that women should learn the lesson so repeatedly taught in the classroom, that boys are brighter than girls.

In the classroom students are constantly gathering fragments of information provided by teachers, to determine *how* they are doing, to construct a picture of their performance and their relation to their peers. One of the fragments of information comes by way of marks and grades. As Goldberg found, and as others including myself have found, teachers frequently think that the contributions of boys are more impressive — not because of the inherent quality of the work, but because they are boys. On five different occasions (and in three countries) I have asked teachers to mark essays, projects, assignments, and I have sometimes indicated that they were by boys and other times that they were by girls. Whenever teachers have assumed they were marking the work of boys, they have consistently

---

* I do not think this equally applicable in secondary schools where groups of boys are often perceived as without intellectual ability, and are frequently allocated to euphemistically labelled 'remedial' classes. Most members of remedial classes are boys and most of the boys are black or working class. In many respects I think that some of these boys have made 'too much trouble' for their teachers, and allocating them to remedial groups is one way of containing and controlling them.

rated it as 'better' than when they have assumed it was written by girls.

I have also found that some funny things happen with the issue of neatness, tidiness or the presentation of the work. Confronted with elaborately prepared projects where much time and attention has been given to setting out the work, teachers are inclined to be contemptuous if they think the work is by a female. Comments such as 'I think she could have spent more time on getting some facts than on making it look pretty' or 'Typical, isn't it? All that effort just to make it look nice — you can't beat girls for being concerned with appearances' were common. But when I indicated that the *same* work was the product of a *boy's* effort, the praise was almost overwhelming: and it wasn't just the presentation that caused comment, for invariably the content, the 'facts', were seen to be more substantial as well.

'When a boy decides to make a thing of it, there's not a girl that can stand up to him' one teacher said of a project on inventions (that he thought was the work of a boy but was actually the work of a girl). The same project when given to other teachers to evaluate was described as 'prissy' and '*She* has not really come to terms with the material.'

But what about the work that was not neat, tidy, and artistically presented? It is fairly obvious that the value system shifts. Untidy and poorly prepared work that was thought to be the effort of a girl was usually penalised — sometimes severely —\whereas untidy and poorly presented work that was thought to be the work of a boy was not penalised and was sometimes praised.

If girls are neat and tidy then their work can be devalued; if girls are untidy and present their material poorly, their work can be devalued. If boys are neat and tidy then their work can be praised and if boys are untidy and present their material poorly their work can still be praised. It is often not the work itself which is being evaluated — but the sex, and according to our beliefs one sex is superior to the other.

This 'fact of life' is understood by both the girls and the boys: it promotes self-confidence and high self-esteem among boys and undermines self-confidence and self-esteem among girls. And it is not difficult to document some of the repercussions.

While it seems that girls can evaluate their own performance in relation to other girls, there are many misapprehensions when girls try to relate their efforts to those of boys, and when boys try to relate their efforts to those of girls.

Girls and boys *do* learn what they are supposed to learn in a patriarchal society, because girls see the boys performing much better than themselves (regardless of the way the boys are performing) and boys see themselves as performing much better than girls (regardless of performance). Girls — and boys — consistently underestimate the abilities and performances of girls and over-estimate the abilities and performances of boys.

Michelle Stanworth conducted her own research on this classroom phenomenon and found in her sample that *all* of the girls *under*-estimated their rank (as supplied by the teacher) in relation to the boys, and that with the exception of one boy, the boys *over*estimated their rank in relation to the girls. In the classroom, says Stanworth, 'boys are indisputably the dominant partners. Girls appear to boys — and more importantly, to themselves — as less capable than they "really" are.' (1981, p40).

The teachers' marks and comments on the students were available to Michelle Stanworth as she interviewed the students. One male student (of whom the history teacher said that his work was not as good as some of the girls), offered the following information, as he sorted through the cards of pupils he rated as better than himself in history.

Male Pupil: I'll put him in as well. Funny actually, it's all boys in that pile.

Interviewer: Strange, isn't it?

Pupil: It's hard to imagine a girl better than me.

Interviewer: Can you imagine? Is it unusual?

Pupil: Yes, I can if I try, maybe, but it *is* unusual. Rosemary — well, I don't know if she's better at History than me, but she is probably better at other subjects, like English, than me. I was at the same school as her for five years, so I know that.

Interviewer: So, can you imagine a girl who is better than you?

Pupil: Yes, I can, but not in History.

Interviewer: Do you think History is more of a man's subject then, in a way?

Pupil: Probably, there's lots of wars in history. That's basically what it's about, why one country's greater than another. And as a rule, girls aren't so good at it.(p42).

The male students indicated to Stanworth that they often did not want to know — for sure — what the girls were doing. They seemed to prefer to retain their illusions without challenge. When asked whether he thought he might compare himself to a girl, Glenda, one boy said 'Not so much Glenda. I think she's doing well; in fact the teacher told me Glenda's doing as well as me. But I wouldn't want to go and look at her essays for instance. Not at a girl's.'

Jenny Shaw (1977) has suggested that there are occasions when the boys do not even take the work of the girls into account and has said 'I remembered talking to a thirteen-year-old boy who said he had come top. He had done very well in his class. It turned out that he had come top of the boys, he hadn't come top of the class overall.' (p57). Denying the existence of girls can make life much simpler, and can help to preserve illusions, for boys.

The girls also often help the boys to keep their illusions: when I interviewed fifteen-year-old girls at one London comprehensive, and asked them if they ever told the boys that they got higher marks, or felt they were more capable, one girl summed it up for all when she said to me, 'What are you, miss? Stupid?'

They all volunteered the information about the way they camouflaged positive performances, if not to all boys, then most definitely to their boyfriends. Most of them stated explicitly that they pretended they were dumb in the presence of boys who 'mattered' and expressed the sentiment that 'it doesn't pay for girls to be too bright.'

This is consistent with findings in the United States where, as early as 1947 and 1949, studies indicated that female students pretended intellectual inferiority when talking to males (Kamarovsky, 1946; Wallen, 1950) and where girls still enhance the image of males at the expense of their own:

'When a girl asks me what mark I got last semester, I answer, "Not so good — only one A." When a boy asks the same question, I say very brightly with a note of surprise, "Imagine, I got an A!"'
(Nancy Frazier and Myra Sadker, 1973; p127).

This raises the issue of 'attribution', an issue currently being explored systematically in the United States, where researchers are concerned with determining what students attribute their success or failure to, and it seems there are sexually different patterns of attribution. In the context of mathematics, Sheila Tobias (1978; b) has found that where girls are successful they often attribute their success to luck, and where they are unsuccessful they often feel that their 'true' aptitude has been ascertained and even use phrases such as 'having been found out'.

Boys also frequently attribute some of their performances to luck and some to 'true' aptitude, but in different ways, for whereas the girls feel they have good luck, the boys feel they have bad luck. Boys who are unsuccessful are more likely to attribute their performance to bad luck, and where successful are more likely to attribute their performance to a reflection of their true ability. Boys approach the task with high self-esteem and 'failure' does not necessarily threaten that self-esteem (indeed, it can even serve as an 'incentive', as a spur to do more work) but girls who approach the task with low self-esteem often feel demoralised by failure — even of a relatively mild form — and it serves to confirm the belief in their own 'deficiency' and can lead them to 'withdraw' rather than to work harder. So, even when the students may get the same marks, girls are likely to interpret its significance differently from boys and consistently with the image of females in society: a high mark means they have been lucky and a low mark that their real aptitude has been demonstrated. On the other hand, boys with high marks are likely to attribute this to their real ability, and consistently with the social image of males to 'explain' a low mark in terms of bad luck, or insufficient work.

It would seem that self-concept plays a major role in the way students interpret their performances, and in the way they set themselves goals, but unfortunately this has never featured as a priority research area. In Britain, Margaret Spencer has done some work in relation to this on reading, and has suggested that people who can visualise themselves as readers, who feel that reading is an appropriate activity for them, are more inclined to learn to read — and to learn more quickly — than those who see reading as something out of reach, unreal, or inappropriate (Spencer and McKenzie, 1975). While this may be equally applicable to being a mathematician or a scientist, few investigations have been undertaken in this country.

In the United States, however, Elizabeth Fennema (1980) has been engaged in research on this particular problem. She has found that (up to a certain age) when asked whether girls are capable of being mathematicians, whether girls like, enjoy, and are competent at mathematics, the girls invariably answer in the affirmative. John Ernest (1976) reports a similar response (which in his research was rather a problem, for the investigation had been initially designed on the premise that girls did not like mathematics and did not feel they were competent). But Fennema went further than Ernest, and asked the *boys* whether *girls* could do mathematics.

The boys said no: girls could not be mathematicians. And during adolescence many of the girls changed their opinions and began to state that girls could not do mathematics. They repudiated their own experience and took on the perspective of boys, when, it seems, they reached the age at which boys' opinions became important. Even where they were prepared to retain the idea that girls *could* do mathematics, many of the girls explained their withdrawal from mathematics classes in terms of 'It's not right; girls can't be mathematicians, can they?'

Male supremacy depends upon males being perceived as superior, and as Virginia Woolf (1974) has said 'Women have served all these centuries as looking-glasses possessing the magic and delicious power of reflecting the figure of man at twice its natural size.' But this is only part of the story for while females are enhancing the image of men, they are also diminishing the image of themselves. They learn to accept the greater authority, ability and significance of men, but they also learn to project the lesser authority, ability and importance of themselves, in order that the differential status between the two sexes can be perceived and preserved. Jenny Shaw (1977) has also commented on this aspect of behaviour as it applies in the classroom and has suggested that girls serve as a *negative reference group* for boys; that is, that not only do they represent a category that boys do not want to be members of (that they 'dislike' and 'despise' as some informed Stanworth), but that the presence of girls is necessary in order to promote the positive image of boys. It is *against* the girls that boys stand out. And classroom dynamics help them to achieve this end.

Teachers and students subscribe to the belief in male superiority, and help it to materialise in the classroom in numerous ways, even though, in Katherine Clarricoates' terms this may amount to the wholesale theft of girls' creativity and intelligence. Of course, classrooms alone are not the only arenas where female creativity and ability is denied by males, or even appropriated by males for their own use. It is a feature of society as a whole.

My own research on language reveals that time and time again, in mixed-sex discussions, the contributions of females are apparently ignored, only to resurface minutes — sometimes seconds — later as a *male* utterance, and then to be treated seriously, and even accorded praise. What, I wonder, is happening? Do males actually not recognise that women have made suggestions which have gone unnoticed, or do they *appropriate* women's suggestions and take them as their own? I would find it difficult to accept that males do not 'hear', that they have generated these ideas on their own, and that the fact that women made them previously was just 'coincidental'. Such an explanation seems unlikely because of the frequency of these incidents, but it also seems unlikely because there is a documented pattern of 'appropriation' of women's ideas in other areas.

Hilary Simpson (1979), for example, has shown how D.H. Lawrence appropriated the writings of women and passed them off as his own. William Wordsworth used Dorothy Wordsworth's diary as the source of many of his ideas and much of his 'inspiration', just as F. Scott Fitzgerald used the diaries of Zelda Fitzgerald. And Marion Glastonbury (1978) indicates that the process continues today, as among many of the respectable male writers, women — usually wives — undertake many of the creative and imaginative tasks (as well as many of the routine and dreary ones) and are acknowledged in two lines while the men stand as the authors.*

Where the creativity of women is seen in general as a service for men, then it is not unlikely that it will make its presence felt in the classroom. When girls exhibit creativity and imagination, and intellectual competence, their behaviour can be filtered through the belief that girls are a *negative* group and that this is no creativity, imagination or competence at all — which perhaps helps to explain why so many males feel no compunction about appropriating women's efforts; but boys are a *positive* group and so what they do *can* be viewed as creative, imaginative, and intellectual — even perhaps when it does not qualify.** And both women and men can play their part in structuring the intellectual supremacy of males, not because of their performance, but because of their sex. In this way women are made to disappear in the classroom and in the records (where they receive only an 'acknowledgement'), women are positioned as wrong, men are perceived as the best candidates, and patriarchy prospers.

Matina Horner (1976) has stated that our society is 'characterized by a general inability to reconcile competence, ambition, intellectual

* Germaine Greer (1980) suggests that a similar pattern has prevailed in the art world.

** These are culturally specific terms and I am dubious about setting up firm categories of creativity, *etc.*

accomplishment and success with femininity. When, for instance, women stray from the image and do use their heads and develop their minds, they are praised for having *masculine minds*' (p44) for the concept of positive intelligence is one that is masculine. Women have been intimidated, states Horner, into accepting that intellectual competence is unfeminine, and that women who display it are not 'proper' women. Traditionally, the penalty of being branded as unfeminine has been sufficient threat to keep women in their place and to coerce them towards feigning 'stupidity'. But such a penalty does not have the force today that it has had in the past, even if only because women have come to recognise that the whole concept of femininity has been decreed by men in their own interest, and has never had its origins in women's experience, despite the number of women who may have tried to fulfil its requirements.

From women's perspective, perhaps it is necessary to revise our theories of learning. Among the objective studies carried out by researchers in the mould of male dominance, the question of boys needing to feel superior in order to learn has never arisen. But confronted with the evidence that boys perform better in mixed-sex schools (see Chapter 9, Single-Sex Schools are Unreal) where girls serve as a negative reference group, against which boys' performance is enhanced, one wonders about possible sex differences in learning. Is it that girls do not need to view their achievement in relation to an inferior group, for this could help to explain why girls do well in single-sex schools and boys do not? It is a possibility worth exploring, but one which might not find popularity in male controlled circles: it could present males in an unflattering light.

The current situation, however, in which girls do act as a negative reference group for boys, and enhance the image and performance of boys, is not inevitable: it can be changed. Women can stop serving as looking-glasses reflecting men at twice their natural size, we can cease to project images of ourselves as less capable and we can start asserting the validity of our own meanings and experiences. So false and fragile is the foundation stone of patriarchy, so much does it depend on the consensus of women, that it cannot but be threatened once we cease to co-operate. Reclaiming our creativity and intelligence is very much in our own hands and within our own grasp. *We* are the ones who will decide what will and will not be 'feminine' and we can begin by asserting that it is very unfeminine to masquerade as dumb or stupid. It is neither inevitable nor mandatory that we should serve as a negative reference group for men.

Part Four
The World According to Men

7 The 'Logic' of Dominance

It is not preordained that schools and education should be arranged in their present form with their deeply entrenched hierarchical structures and their primary role of separating those who qualify from those who do not. Nor is it mandatory that schools and education should function on the premise that the inequalities which abound in society are the consequences of different inherent aptitudes (which are of course simply measured by the agents of education in 'neutral' fashion). It is not inevitable that schools should accept inequality as something which 'naturally unfolds' rather than divisions which have been cultivated. We can see how schools help to create these inequalities and we can modify their practices. Schools *could* serve to challenge some of the existing premises, and education *could* be a powerful force for social change and for the construction of a more egalitarian society. It could be . . .

But being in a dominant position has its own seductive logic and it is profitable to see how and why this logic operates, particularly if we wish to challenge it. It is the dominant group which has decreed most of the present arrangements in which their dominance is realised, and the arrangements therefore are likely to please them, to be seen as sensible, to receive their sanction and approval. Those who occupy the top positions in society, who enjoy benefits and privileges derived from their position, do not have to be malicious to suspect that the means whereby they gained their status and benefits were legitimate, and that there is something wrong with those at the bottom who have not achieved the same success.

If members of the dominant group assert that the way is open and that there are no impediments to entry to their privileged circle (except of course in terms of ability) then it is quite likely that they are accurately describing their own experience of the world. What they leave out of course is that their experience is not the only experience, although their power permits them to pass it off as the only legitimate experience. They leave out the explanation that they are the ones deemed to have ability — because they are the ones who decide what constitutes ability.

If members of the dominant group feel they have been treated fairly by a system in which they have succeeded, it is only a slight shift for them to generalise that the system is fair to all. They may be genuinely puzzled by accusations that education and schooling are discriminatory — for after all, this was not their particular experience — and they may find it beyond their comprehension to understand that not all students are supported, encouraged, validated and helped to realise their potential. When some members of society who are not members of the dominant group describe their educational experiences as constricting, discouraging, rejecting, then rather than question their own experience and their own role it may be easier and more logical for the dominant group to explain this discrepancy in terms of those who have not met their standards, to 'blame the victims' and conclude that such protests and complaints are 'sour grapes', evidence of bitterness.

How often do policy and decision makers — and many teachers — state emphatically and unequivocally that students are treated fairly, that there is equality of educational opportunity, and that they themselves are part of the evidence that it works? And it is not uncommon for them to take their logic one step further and to argue that if remedial reading classes are full of black boys, and if girls do not take up mathematics and science, it is the limitations of the students themselves which must be held accountable.

Repeatedly when I have tried to assert that the fault lies not with the students, but the system in which they find themselves, I have been met by responses which range from bewilderment to hostility, as members of the powerful group explain — from their position and experience of power — that the system is open and fair, and that it is beyond dispute that certain students do not meet the necessary standards.

But where do these standards come from? Who made them up and for what reasons? They are not neutral standards, nor are they absolute. They vary over time and place. They were not simply waiting in the world for men to discover them. They are standards set by the dominant group, they originate in their perspective on the world, and they serve their interests.

I do not dispute the validity of that experience for those who are dominant: what I do dispute is that their experience of the world is the *only* experience, their standards the *only* standards. Those who share neither their power nor their experience could very easily set different 'standards'. It would not be difficult to transform today's 'failures' into tomorrow's successes if the power base were to be changed. Sometimes, history is a record of this very process in action as the power shifts and a new crop of 'best candidates' emerges with different qualities necessary to meet the new standards.

If there is to be a dominant group in society, and its dominance is to be accepted (as distinct from imposed by brute force) and agreed to be reasonable, then a suitable mechanism must be devised to justify dominance. If men are to be accepted as the dominant sex (or whites as the dominant race), then they must be able to 'prove' that they are in some way superior, hence their dominance is deserved. If they can establish that they are better, then it is only right and reasonable that they should get the best jobs.

Schools, and other educational institutions in which men order the values and structure experience, serve as one of the mechanisms which help to 'prove' that men are indeed superior and therefore, quite rightly, get the bigger and better share of the cake. When the world is divided into public and private, into paid and unpaid labour, for example, and when the public world of paid work is perceived as more prestigious and can bestow considerable benefits, then educational institutions help to 'prove' in many ways that males are more suited to one than to the other. Males reach the required standards for the prestigious and paid work much more frequently than do females, so it is quite legitimate that they should hold these positions in much greater numbers.

Likewise, the standards set for women, by men, are standards that males often fail to meet. It is impossible, say many teachers, for many boys to be quiet, tidy and conformist, to be co-operative and conciliatory, to undertake tedious and routine chores, to wait upon others and be responsible — particularly emotionally and psychologically — for others. This is one of the reasons boys are supposedly no good at housework.

When I have asked teachers whether males should be involved in housework and childcare, I have received the following responses which I consider fairly representative (from those who do not class themselves as feminists):

> 'I think it's demeaning for a man to do housework and also, probably, worse to look after children. I'd have no respect for a man who did it and I think it would be terrible if boys had to learn about it in school.

> If parents want their sons to be cissies then they'll have to teach them themselves because they are sure as hell not going to be taught that here.

I think men should be able to help their wives, and also take over in emergencies. I think it would be a good idea for boys to have some idea about housework and childcare and I think they could have short courses in school. Although I can understand why the boys wouldn't like it. It would probably have to be compulsory.

It's personal choice and shouldn't be associated with school. Some boys might want to know more about the domestic scene, and good for them. But they can learn outside school. It's not the sort of thing the school should teach, there's no intellectual skills involved. If we spent half our time teaching the kids domestic things we wouldn't have time for all the proper work. It would really lower our educational standards.'

So, it is demeaning for a man to engage in housework and childcare, it is 'cissy' and stigmatised, it is undesirable activity which by choice boys would not want to spend their time in. It is perhaps something they should be able to do in an emergency, or to help those whose daily life it is and who might be overburdened, but you wouldn't want boys doing it in school because it would lower the standards!

(These four teachers all claimed to treat the sexes equally.)

What is good for the goose is certainly not good for the gander it seems: it is alright for girls to learn about housework and childcare, it is alright for them to be channelled into accepting that it is their lot in life, but there is enormous resistance to the idea that boys should engage in or be trained in the same role. They are not suitable for it, it is not suitable for them. Men have structured and interpreted housework and childcare as a non-rewarding activity, have allocated it to women, 'proved' that women are more suited to its demeaning demands and that because of this, they are handicapped when it comes to the world of public, paid, prestigious work. By such means is the superiority of the male established.

The logic of dominance is such that those who have power can choose their successors in their own image and they can choose those who have a vested interest in perpetuating the same system and reproducing the same patterns of inequality that have served them so well; their choice, they can genuinely argue, is neither partial nor prejudiced, it is not sex discrimination — can they help it if it so happens that males are superior? It is not their fault, so they say.

It cannot be disputed that in our society education is a resource and that students emerge from the educational process with that resource most unevenly distributed and according to perfectly predictable patterns (which are not confined to sex). Males do better than females, they get more of this resource over all, more in the highly prestigious areas which correlate with financial rewards, more opportunities to gain and to use this resource (see also Eileen Byrne, 1978). When the educational outcome is so demonstrably unequal the question arises as to how this distribution can be accepted as logical and fair.

One way that it has been possible to pass off this result as fair (by those who provide the logic and the explanations) is by the insistence that schools, for example, play a passive role, merely recording the interests and aptitudes of students through the use of impartial tests and standards, through the provision of options from which students may freely choose, through neutral counselling which takes into account the needs and interests of the students.

In the nurturing environment of the school, so the argument goes, the nature of the sexes merely unfolds and is recognised by the school. The school is not responsible for this pattern of development, it merely provides the context in which it emerges.

While this may be a logical description and explanation for those who emerged as 'naturally' superior and whose growth and development was fostered and facilitated along the way, it is not the description and explanation of those who emerged as 'naturally' inferior. In three classes of college students that I have taught, I have asked the female students to write their educational autobiographies and *without exception* the most salient feature remembered by all was the sense of activities and aspirations that were forbidden (see also Phillipa Brewster, 1980, *School Days, School Days*).

In commenting on nineteenth century education, Gerda Lerner (1977) has stated that 'For American boys the world was theirs to explore, to tame, to conquer; for girls the home was to be the world. For American boys the development of a strong individuality and strong will was a necessary value preparing them for their roles. For girls, the subduing of the will, the acceptance of self-abnegation, and the development of excessive altruism were the desired educational goals' (p3) and 'more frequently than the boy she would experience growing up as a loss, a confinement, a decrease of freedom' (p5).

The experience of contemporary girls growing up in Britain seems to share some similarities with their American predecessors, for 'confinement', 'restriction', 'forbidden' were commonly used words. 'I wanted to do law, but I wasn't allowed', 'They wouldn't let me do physics', 'I was stopped from being boisterous and having a good time', 'It was always what I can't do, never what I could do and after everything was ruled out of bounds there wasn't much left.'

Glenys Lobban (1977) and Camilla Nightingale (1977) have tried to establish some of the messages that are conveyed to girls and boys within the school and have used books as an index. Their work corroborates the experience articulated by girls. 'Adventure books written especially for boys have a far wider scope than those for girls' says Nightingale. 'Boys' books are about subjects like trapping, sailing, smuggling, mining, the Wild West, cops and robbers. Scenes are set all over the world from Alaska to The South China Seas. The boy heroes need not only physical courage, they need to know what they are doing in great technical detail. Books like these are there to expand a boy's horizons. Read a corresponding book for girls and you will conclude it is expressly designed to dampen down any spirit a girl may have left.' (p98).

It may be that such an educational experience for males feels free, unfettered and fair. It may even be that they feel they are merely unfolding, developing their full potential. But this is not the case for many girls, particularly those educated in mixed-sex contexts. It is not their experience that education opens up the world to them and encourages them to expand. Rather, many girls have the feeling that their schooling played a crucial role in confining their expectations, restricting their interests, limiting their potential. To them, school played an active, not a passive role in their development. Boys may feel they were born but girls have the distinct feeling they were made. This is another case where the 'logic' of dominance is not so defensible when it is juxtaposed against the 'logic' of those who are dominated.

It would not be difficult to arrange schooling so that there was genuine equality and so that students did emerge with equal resources. There are, however, arguments provided by the dominant group against such arrangements. One argument has remained much the same for centuries and it is that if females had other options, they would be disinclined to marry. With this I would concur, but it is more an argument for changing marriage (in my frame of reference) than for coercing females into it.

Another argument is that we would eradicate many of the current sex differences, and for those who profit from the present arrangement it can be seen why such an eventuality would be undesirable. The present power base would be undermined if it were no longer possible to prove that males were superior and therefore justified in claiming the realm of paid work in the public sphere. According to the logic of the dominant group there could well be anarchy if the sexes possessed equal resources and assumed equal responsibility for servicing their own lives and those of their offspring.

Currently, we accept the word of men that they are the better students, the more suitable applicants for paid work, the best candidates for positions of power and influence; we accept their word that there would be a breakdown in the family, in society, if their form of order were to be abandoned. The question is whether we should continue to accept their word, whether their logic is sufficiently logical, whether we should start to voice and validate our own experience and our own logic?

Perhaps males are realising more of their potential under present arrangements — although of this I am not convinced, given that males have defined potential and success and they appear to me most lopsided definitions — but consider the extent of the preferential treatment they receive. The system is designed for them, it fits their experience of the world, it teaches and legitimates that experience. From my perspective it seems logical to suggest that girls would emerge equally as qualified (in men's terms) if they were to receive the same advantageous treatment.

Of course, for girls to receive the same advantages as boys would entail many changes in schooling. They would need a system designed for them and one which validated and reinforced their own version of experience. They would need knowledge by and about women. They would need to devise their own 'standards'. And education would look very different — as it does in many women's studies courses where females are in control of their own learning.

That this constitutes such an 'unrealistic' possibility is a measure of the extent of sexism in education, for what constitutes the daily educational reality for the male sex, borders on fantasy for the female sex.

I do not envisage an 'overnight revolution' which would put the control of women's education (and some of the education of men) into women's hands, but I can envisage an evolution where women begin to exercise some influence and where they do so according to their own logic.

My own very limited interventions (and those of other feminists) indicate that it takes less amounts of time, energy and organisation to open up horizons than it does to close them. Sometimes a simple question may be sufficient — for example, who does the talking in your class? Why are all the books about males? What will you be doing when you are thirty? — and may produce results that are little short of astonishing as the frame of reference for making sense of the world shifts rapidly in the space of seconds. The answers to these particular questions are not as important as the direction in which they lead, as students begin to ask how and why it was that they have not noticed these things before.

Such questions can produce change, not the sort of change that is perceived as a revolution and attained by violent means (and we need to question the origin of this particular model of change) but the sort of evolutionary change that accompanies a reconceptualisation of the world.

This type of change which is associated with redefining and re-evaluating the objects and events of the world *is* genuine learning. It is the same sort of exercise that Galileo engaged in when he reconceptualised the relationship of the earth to the solar system, and the same thing that Darwin was doing when he reconceptualised the origin of human beings. It was also what Mary Wollstonecraft did when she pointed out that women were second-class citizens precisely because men engineered this particular relationship, and what Germaine Greer (1971) did when she stated that women were made not born, and that there was nothing at all 'normal' about the sex roles we learn to play from our infancy; when men engage in this activity it is usually called learning and theorising, but when women engage in it, to analyse women's experience, it is more often than not today called consciousness-raising. And according to male logic, consciousness-raising is *not* a genuine learning activity, on the contrary it is some form of political/emotional behaviour which has no place in the properly impersonal and detached learning environment.

It may well be the male view that the learning in which they are engaged is more significant, more reliable, more impersonal, detached and objective, for this reality is sustained throughout the whole of society. To men it may seem that when women begin to articulate their experience and to conceptualise the world from their perspective, they are engaging in a trivial, irrational — and sometimes even a political — activity. But women do not always share this view. To women it may seem that the concentration on male experience to the exclusion of all else, the necessary reverence demanded for male experience and authority, and the emotional protests made by men when proposals for change are introduced, amount to nothing less than an irrational and political response to women's reason and logic.

The logic of women and men, viewed in this way, may be different, even contradictory, but nonetheless equally valid. The reason that one version is commonly acceptable and the other is not, is because one group has the power to impose its version of experience on members of society who share neither the experience nor the logic. This does not make it right or just.

If women's experience and logic were to be equally valued and valid, if they were to coexist with men's, we would have a very different society and very different schools. Male experience could no longer be perceived as the sum total of human experience and males would be in the position of having to listen, some of the time, to women, instead of the present situation where women are required almost all of the time to listen to men (see Pamela Fishman, 1977, who documents the 'linguistic availability' of women). Men could no longer be the sole authorities, much of their rationale for their own supremacy (and their rationale that women are wrong) would no longer be appropriate. The 'logic' of male dominance would be exposed as most illogical if women were to be taken into account.

It is primarily because I wish to see the realisation of sexual equality that I advocate that women take and use every opportunity to articulate their own experience, to describe and explain the world in the way it impinges on women, and this includes speaking of male dominance and the methods it uses to silence and discredit women. I am advocating that all women demand some control over some of their education, that they insist on the right to learn more about their own lives, and that they cease to care whether men label it learning or consciousness-raising. The false logic of dominance demands too high a price and can no longer be afforded.

8 The Blank Future

Being a woman is inextricably linked in the minds of most members of our society with being a wife and mother. While parenthood applies equally to both sexes, however, the meanings that are attributed to it are sexually differentiated, so that being a female parent — a mother — is viewed as a very different role from being a male parent — a father. Motherhood is perceived as an ongoing activity, which begins, rather than ends, with the birth of a child, and which demands years of a woman's life; whereas fatherhood is often confined to the mechanics of conception, is a discrete activity which demands very little time. While reproduction is seen as central in women's lives — and is often believed to be the means by which women become 'fulfilled' — it is usually viewed as peripheral for men, it is an 'extra' and not a necessary condition of existence.

Many educational philosophies have been based on the premise that a good education is one which fits students for their place in the world, one which equips them for their future life; and while men have conceptualised women's future in terms of motherhood (and men's in terms of employment) it has seemed 'logical' to provide education for motherhood for girls, and education for employment for boys. To many educationalists such a policy is 'sensible' and they refuse to acknowledge that it is discriminatory and plays a role in ensuring the subordination of women to men. It is the 'same old story'; women are denied certain knowledge (on the grounds that they are women) and then 'blamed' because they do not possess the same knowledge as men.

This policy of sexually differentiated and discriminatory provision is evident in virtually every official educational report that has ever been presented (see Carol Dyhouse, 1976, 1977, 1978, and Marion Scott, 1980, for further discussion) and far from being the prejudice of the past, is a characteristic feature of current educational philosophy, for the prerogative to formulate 'sound' educational principles still remains firmly in the hands of men. *The Norwood Report* of 1943 stated that girls should have a knowledge of domestic subjects for it was 'necessary equipment for all girls as potential makers of homes' and while boys — the 'better' students — could tackle the rigorous, theoretical subjects, girls could engage in domestic subjects because they 'have the advantage of offering a practical approach to theoretical work'.* *The Newsom Report* (1963) also stated unequivocally that 'For *all* girls' (my emphasis) 'there is a group of interests relating to what many, perhaps most of them, would regard as their most important vocational concern, marriage', and it followed, therefore, that their education should capitalise on this interest in their vocation and make available subjects which were related to homemaking and child-rearing.

It seems that little has changed since Rousseau insisted that the purpose behind the education of girls was to make them attractive to men — 'attractive' in physical terms (and many current domestic science courses include 'grooming' and 'fashion', and the emphasis is not usually on health) and 'attractive' in terms of their ability to look after men.** Today, many educationalists start with the premise that girls *should* make motherhood their vocation, and they then proceed to educate them for that vocation — which necessitates eliminating many other options — and then the same educationalists stand triumphant and vindicated, when most female graduates of the education system go on to be mothers, and to make motherhood a vocation. Some even go so far as to assert that the girls *willingly chose* motherhood as the central factor in their existence, for while every educational opportunity is 'equally open to girls', they argue the girls *choose* to see paid employment as secondary and not plan their lives in terms of its requirements.

Very few educationalists recognise the part they play in making these things 'come true' for women. They do not see themselves as actively depriving women of a range of options, as actively preventing women from attaining economic independence, as actively loading the dice against women so that many settle on motherhood by default.

This is not to denigrate motherhood. Giving birth to children is fundamentally necessary to any society, and rearing children can be

* It could be argued that metalwork, woodwork, engineering, *etc.,* could equally well offer a practical approach to theoretical work but this did not appear nearly so 'sensible' an arrangement.

** During the 1980 Miss World Contest, the announcers on one London Radio Station prepared a Form Guide but also discussed the fact that the competitors were not asked the real, most important and fundamental question of how well they could look after men!

one of the most crucial and valuable tasks undertaken in any society. But in our society, where men have made up the rules, they have allocated child-rearing to women and treated it as trivial; they have also made it a difficult and at times impossible task, by insisting that it be unpaid, unshared and unsupported. If women do perceive the value and the reward of child-rearing and do *choose freely* to undertake the difficult task, we should be encouraged, assisted and even admired; but for many of us it is no choice at all, it is an expectation that we fulfil because it seems that there is nothing else available. Bombarded from birth with the message that we must be mothers, channelled through our education to plan our futures in terms of child-rearing rather than employment, settling on occupations that are frequently a fill-in till life supposedly begins with our man, our home, and our children, many of us may find ourselves mothers, without ever having seriously considered any other alternative. Scared by stories about spinsters, frightened by fairy tales of unfulfilment, lured by love and romance, we move optimistically towards the destiny men have decreed for us, and find frequently that we are dependent and subordinate, that we have become the next generation of women to support and perpetuate male dominance.

It is not necessary to embark on a vast research project in order to find out how this 'con-trick' was, and is, perpetrated. That women do not perceive any alternatives is partly because they are not there: men have removed the evidence. Women are given only one side of the story — the men's side — and it is in men's interest that we go on seeing our role in life as one of pleasing and looking after men. Few of us know that in 1739 'Sophia, A Person of Quality' wrote a pamphlet, *Woman Not Inferior to Man*, in which she said that if '... every individual man (were) to divulge his thoughts of our sex, they would all be unanimous in thinking, that we are made for their use, that we are fit only to breed and nurse children in their tender years, to mind household affairs, and to obey, serve and please our masters, *themselves*, forsooth.' 'Sophia' went on to say why this was absurd, unjust, and could only be the view of men. Having been confronted with the argument that learning and education were wasted on women, because they only married and had children, Sophia exposed the ludicrous logic of this argument: 'Why is *learning* useless to us? Because we have no share in public offices. And why have we no share in public offices? Because we have no *learning*.'

If in the course of education girls — and boys — were required to study Sophia, and Mary Astell who worked for the establishment of a women's college, Priscilla Wakefield, who wrote children's books, popularised natural history, and started savings banks, Mary Somerville, who translated Newton's work for lay people and was one of the leading scientists of her time, Ada Lovelace, who developed computer software (the significance of which was not realised until relatively recently), Sophia Jex Beake, who fought the medical profession, Christabel Pankhurst, who fought the politicians, and the many thousands of other possibly 'meaningless' women who could be cited, then both sexes would graduate from school knowing that for hundreds of years there has been a coherent criticism of male dominance. Both sexes would know the arguments *against* male control as well as being versed in the reasons for that control. Women would then be in a position to *choose* between independence and dependence. The fears of men that they may choose independence, that they may reject the present arrangements of marriage and motherhood which make women dependent (see Rich, 1980) might be well founded. This is one of the reasons that knowledge about these women — and their protests against male dominance — is not readily available.

Many are the mechanisms designed to ensure that such knowledge does not get into the hands of women, particularly young, impressionable women students. Numerous are the teachers who can testify that attempts to bring such knowledge about women's strength and the history of women's protest into the classroom are classified by many authorities as *propaganda*. While almost the entire curriculum is about men, the inclusion of a few women can be perceived as political and subversive.

In one sense, those who assert that it is political and subversive for students to study women are right, for once women come to understand that there has been a female philosophical tradition, a tradition of analysis and criticism of male power and female dependence, women are subverted from the present arrangements in which men prosper. But men have left something out of their argument — they have not stated that it is political and subversive to study women in a male dominated society, they have not stated that women are only free to choose from the options that men provide and are not free to decide for themselves.

While males retain control of society they control the options that are available to women, and whether women *choose* to seek male approval or to dispense with it (as women without men) they can find themselves penalised. For even choosing male approval exacts a price under the present arrangements where those who conform to the 'desired' pattern and become wives and mothers, as those roles are currently structured, almost always find themselves financially dependent; in our monetary society financial dependence can lead to many other forms of dependence and women's options can be even further reduced. Women who have 'chosen' this role frequently perceive their future as non-existent, as blank.

When I was about seventeen, and perceived as difficult, maladjusted and ungrateful, my mother tried genuinely to help me. '*Who* do you want to be like?' she asked. 'Just tell me *who* and I'll do my best to help you.' We made a list of the women we knew, and among them were teachers, secretaries and hairdressers. But even these women who did have paid jobs, still defined themselves primarily as *housewives* and their paid jobs as 'something extra' to 'help out'. I didn't want to be like any of them, with no identity of my own, no independence of my own.

So we turned to literature — or at least to our limited knowledge of literature. Jane Austen's Emma was discounted, Anna Karenina and Madame Bovary were discounted, Lady Macbeth and Ophelia were discounted — and who was left? After our systematic search for a 'model' we agreed that there was no-one that I wanted to be like, that what I wanted was unreal, that it simply didn't exist. *All* women, as far as we could see, became housewives or else encountered most unfortunate ends. Be a housewife and mother —or draw a blank.

There have been some changes in twenty years. It is possible today to suggest a range of women models, some of whom meet men's terms and even some who meet women's terms, but they are not the *norm*. The expectation is still that women's proper sphere is the home, that women cannot function adequately in the public realm; that some women *do*, is interpreted to mean that they are *unrepresentative* of their sex, not that the beliefs about the female sex are inaccurate. And women who do enter the public realm often encounter hostility and abuse, they are often the object of 'jokes' and 'witticisms' based on the premise that this is not their proper place. No man is ever urged to return to the dishes, because it is not expected that that is where he has come from.

That women are seen as wives and mothers first and foremost in our society is not difficult to substantiate, but because this is one of the major means by which women are made subordinate, and because many educationalists profess that they wish to change the dependence of women and to provide 'equality of opportunity' for both sexes, we might expect to find that teachers were trying to provide positive alternatives to motherhood and marriage as the sole goals for women. It seems, however, that this is not the case, that there are some teachers who staunchly defend the division of labour based on sex, and who provide 'sensible' education for these ends, while many, many other teachers who may not actively promote motherhood as the exclusive realm for women, commit the sin of omission — if not a mother then there is nothing but a blank.

It would be misguided to believe that it is only male teachers who see women primarily as wives and mothers (with short term paid employment initially, and part-time paid employment, perhaps, after the children go to school), for women teachers are victims as well, and often have difficulty in perceiving their female students in any other terms. One woman teacher, interviewed by Michelle Stanworth (1981), described a very competent and efficient female student:

Female Teacher: I can imagine her being a very competent, if somewhat detached secretary. She looks neat and tidy, her work's neat and tidy, she's perfectly prompt at arriving. And she moves round with an air of knowing what she's doing. She doesn't drift.

Interviewer: Why would she be a *detached* secretary?

Teacher: I can't imagine her falling for her boss at all! Or getting in a flap.

Interviewer: What about in five years time?

Teacher: Well, I can see her having a family, and having them jolly well organised. They'll get up at the right time and go to school at the right time, wearing the right clothes. Meals will be ready when her husband gets home. She'll handle it jolly well. (p26).

The woman student in question was actually considering enrolling for a law degree — but if she does so, it will be against the implicit and explicit advice and expectations of some of her teachers. (Stanworth herself states that the student is perfectly capable of doing a university degree.) Students rely heavily on the advice and assessment of teachers, and it is difficult for them to ignore such advice; but when this advice and expectation is added to the doubts which are systematically instilled in girls, and when these are added to the overwhelming *lack* of evidence that it is proper for a girl to do a university degree, particularly a law degree, it would not be surprising if this student 'chose' to be a secretary, perhaps a legal secretary. What is surprising is that so many women are not sensible, that they defy the evidence of our society, and that they go on to commit themselves to paid employment and to make provisions for such commitment.

However, while the women teachers in Stanworth's sample had some (albeit traditional) ideas about women's futures in the world of work, 'it is almost as if the working lives of women are a mystery to men' states Stanworth, for 'in two-thirds of male teachers' discussion of female pupils, the girl could not be envisaged in *any* occupation once her education was complete' (p27, my emphasis).

Male Teacher: She would be competent enough to do a course at a university or polytechnic, though not necessarily the most academic course.

Interviewer: What sort of course might suit her then?

Teacher: I can't say. I don't really know about jobs for girls.

*   *   *   *   *   *   *

Male Teacher: She will probably go on to further or higher education. You'd know better than I what a young girl with an independent mind might be doing in five years. (p28).

In psychological, sociological and educational studies it has been amply demonstrated that for all of us the expectations of others play a significant role in our lives. We should not underestimate the importance of *absence* of expectation in terms of women students; that teachers have so many (positive) expectations for boys, so many diverse expectations for their better students and so few expectations for girls could well be crucial. Boys so often receive information that a variety of jobs are open to them and it is appropriate that they should plan for them, but so often girls receive the information that *nothing* is available, that the future is a blank; if it is to have any shape they must shape it for themselves, and on their own, with neither guidance nor encouragement.

What is expected of girls is that they be supportive of the efforts and achievements of boys: among the sample Stanworth interviewed there was one student who was ranked as the best performer in both her main subjects, but when asked what she would be doing in the future, her teacher envisaged her as 'personal assistant to someone rather important'. (p28).

Once more we can see that what is done is not as important as which sex does it. Teachers are simply showing another aspect of those attitudes mentioned earlier; boys are expected to achieve more, and in more diverse areas (and, crucially, more remunerative areas) than girls.

These expectations are not hidden in the classroom. They are not even subtle messages conveyed through the substream of interaction. They are more frequently the substance of information that is daily and freely given to girls — and boys. In a mathematics class:

Female Student: Please sir, I can't do question 4. I don't know what it means. Can I have some help?

Male Teacher: Oh don't worry about it, Karen. It's a bit difficult. You won't ever need to know it. (London comprehensive, 1978).

In a history class:

Female Student: But why did they go to war? They didn't really have a reason. It seems such a stupid thing to have done.

Male Teacher: Yes, well I don't expect *you* would understand. It's the men who make these decisions and they had lots of reasons, didn't they? *(Appealing to the boys).* That's why women look after the home and men look after the nation. *(Laughter).* (Outer London comprehensive, 1978).

Female students are systematically informed that they have a sphere, that it is limited and they are limited. Marriage and motherhood are seen as central in that sphere, and neither marriage nor motherhood is seen as an aid or advantage for paid employment. It is almost an absurd idea to suggest that a woman might get married and that this might help her in her paid job— but it is not at all absurd in relation to a man; despite the fact that both are human, both may be equally able, both married, and both wanting to work, both wanting to be independent individuals. Employment is seen as integral to male identity but peripheral to female, and marriage and parenthood as integral to female identity but peripheral to male, and education both reflects and *creates* this belief.

Most of women's dependence has its origins in economic dependence: women earn less than 10% of the world's salaries and own less than 1% of the world's wealth (UN official statistics) and it is very difficult to be contrary when one depends on men for food and shelter. There can be no doubt that in education in general and schools in particular women are encouraged to choose a vocation which — not coincidentally — helps to make them economically dependent. Such dependence helps to ensure that male authority is minimally challenged.

For themselves, men have 'built childcare into the system', they have freed themselves of this responsibility by allocating it exclusively to women, and, of course, they have not seen fit to pay for this service (as women must do when we want our children cared for) but have deemed it a 'labour of love'. Not only can men help to make women economically dependent by this process (with all the concomitant advantages that such dependence can have for men) they can also use it as another reason for arguing that women with children are not the best candidates for the jobs, if and when women do enter the paid workforce.

Because women have to do the male share of childcare, as well as their own, men can use this against women and maintain that women with children are not dependable members of the workforce. If women were to play a part in shaping the values of society they might well argue that both sexes should play an equal part in parenting and then both sexes could enter the paid workforce on equal terms — but of course we would not have the patriarchal society we know today if this were to happen.

There are volumes devoted to the male experience of work (far less about the male experience of marriage and fatherhood), to the transition from school to work, to further education, the workplace, to stress and redundancy, but there are few volumes devoted to what happens to women when they 'choose' to make paid employment secondary (although often essential), and to become wives and mothers, working a double shift.

Jessie Bernard (1972) has stated that marriage makes women sick: 'There are two marriages' she says, 'in every marital union, his and hers. And his ... is better than hers.' (p14). While 'for centuries men have been told — by other men — that marriage is: no bed of roses, a necessary evil, a noose, a desperate thing, a field of battle, a curse ...' *etc.,* it is men who thrive on marriage (p16). 'Despite all the jokes about marriage in which men indulge, all the complaints they lodge against it, it is one of the greatest boons of their sex.' (p17). And, says Jessie Bernard, *men know this*:

'The actions of men with respect to marriage speak far louder than words; they speak in fact with a deafening roar. Once men have known marriage they can hardly live without it. Most divorced and widowed men remarry. At every age, the marriage rate for both divorced and widowed men is higher than the rate for single men. Half of all divorced white men who remarry do so within three years of divorce. Indeed, it might not be far-fetched to conclude that the verbal assaults on marriage indulged in by men are a kind of compensatory reaction to their dependence on it.' (p18). Men do well out of marriage and not surprisingly encourage women to enter it; but what about women?

Looking at the mental health of wives, Jessie Bernard reports that the picture is very grim. The statistics vary from country to country in the Western world but overall the people who are most likely to suffer from depression, who are likely to have breakdowns and be dependent on drugs — are wives. (This stress has not received as much attention, of course, as the stress endured by men in the workforce, despite the fact that mental ill health is greater among those whose occupation is housewife than among any other occupational group.)

Jessie Bernard has proposed a shock theory of marriage, that is, 'that marriage introduces such profound discontinuities in the lives of women as to constitute genuine emotional health hazards.' (p37). So great is the discrepancy between the ideal and the reality that women experience 'shock' which can manifest itself in terms of depression and despair. The ideal, however, persists because the reality gets dismissed frequently as the problem of individual women, and as this does not constitute a problem for men, it is not systematically taken up as a problem for society.

Women who have accepted the man-made myths about marriage are frequently very quickly disillusioned. Firstly they may find that it is they who have to make most of the concessions, partly because they are not in a position to negotiate. 'Because the wife has put so many eggs into the one basket of marriage, to the exclusion of almost every other' says Bernard, 'she has more at stake in making a go of it. If anything happens to that one basket, she loses everything; she has no fallback position.' (p40). She may also find that being a wife means being a *house*wife and that regardless of any paid employment she may be engaged in, she is expected to be the home-maker — the euphemism for cleaner, shopper, cook, *etc.*, an unpaid servant for her husband.

For some women this may be no great surprise, whereas for others it may be complete disillusionment, but for both groups it is often perceived as the *only* possibility, the only avenue open to women. And yet it is an occupation that is fraught with emotional hazards. 'If we were ... epidemiologists' (studying epidemics) says Bernard, 'and saw bright, promising young people enter a certain occupation and little by little droop, and finally succumb, we would be alerted at once and bend all our research efforts to locate the hazards and remove them. But we are complacent when we see what happens to women in marriage.' (p48). It would be dramatically different if it were to happen to men.

Perhaps it is because it *is* understood that marriage makes women sick, that so much effort is expended in enticing women into it (witness the effort of the media), and so much care is taken to reduce or eliminate other options. That other options have been eliminated for women — in psychological and material terms — is beyond dispute. Even those women who do try to give paid employment a central focus in their lives, and who try to plan accordingly, have to plan how they will organise their homes and their children as well, for few young girls aim for and dream of being women alone, of spinsterhood or single parenting, while males control the social reality. When outlining their plans for the future few boys are asked what arrangements they will make for their families, but few girls escape such solicitous questions.

Most of the one hundred schoolgirls I have interviewed see their futures primarily as wives and mothers; only three said they were planning to remain single because they thought they would have a better life. When I asked the one hundred girls how they saw themselves at thirty, however, sixty-four of them said they didn't know — the future was blank. They could see themselves as wives and mothers, but understandably they could also see that this was a temporary occupation, that it finished early, and because it was the *only* occupation they envisaged for themselves there was no replacement image or role when the model of the 'attractive young wife and mother' expired. For many of the young women there was life before thirty plus a vague vision of grandmother, but no in-between. The only role they could conceive for themselves was with children, either their own or their children's children.

Among the sixty-four for whom there was nothing after thirty, only four acknowledged the significance of their own admissions: it is interesting to note that for these four, the simple act of asking them what they would be doing/being after thirty served to promote a whole new range of ideas and plans — although I do not know how long they would have been able to sustain them. I do know, however, that it is often neither a difficult nor complex task to expose the 'con-trick', and 'con-tricks' have a habit of not working once people know they are being 'conned'.

However, for the sixty young women for whom the future was circumscribed as wife and mother, who accepted the definition of women in terms of reproduction, there was basically only a blank in between the birth of their own children and the birth of their children's children. When young women perceive life ending at thirty (in contrast to beginning at forty for men) they are providing a fairly accurate portrayal of the role they are expected to play under patriarchy. They are also pointing to the time they are likely to be at great risk, in terms of their health, when they are literally left with neither a socially valid purpose nor function at a relatively early age.

Dominant explanations of these phenomena are of course very different. All young wives could be depressed and this could continue to be a problem of individual women: all wives over thirty could be desperately sick and this too could still be perceived as a problem of individual women (their own menopausal fault), for the problems of women are not, and never have been, the problems of society. This is why young women repeatedly resolve the contradictions between what they are *told* about the joys of marriage and motherhood, and what they often *know*, by laying the blame on individual women. When asked what they would be doing after thirty, many of the young women I interviewed stated vehemently that they wouldn't be like their mums.

'Not like my mum. I won't be like her. I'll be better organised. I'm not living like that.

I couldn't live like me mum. I want more out of life. I won't make the mess she has.

I'll marry someone with a better job than me dad. More money and security. I'm not going to work like me mum does, and take what she does.'

The comments that the girls made seemed very negative to me — although others might provide a different interpretation. But there were virtually no positive or constructive responses to the question of life after thirty, if one discounts — as I did — comments such as 'I'll probably live in the country' or 'I'll have a really nice, cosy place.'

Student: I'll have a nice husband and three children . . . and a fitted kitchen.

Interviewer: But what will you be, what will your life be like?

Student: Oh, it will be good. I'll have everything I want.

The most common type of response was generalised to all women and there were few individual variations: 'What do you mean, what will I be doing after thirty? What everyone does I suppose.' Some of the responses, however, were not just blank, but bleak:

'After thirty? I don't know. What do girls do after thirty? Just go on, I suppose. It's done by thirty, it's all over then, isn't it?'

While many frames of reference exist in patriarchal society to 'blame' women for many of the structures and conditions that men have devised, I am not providing these examples for that purpose. I am suggesting that the girls are being *realistic* and the fault lies not with them but with an education system and a society that defines them in terms of reproduction — and nothing else — despite the fact that even the way it is currently organised in our society child-bearing and child-rearing may actually demand very few years of their life.

The girls' responses to questions about paid employment are equally realistic and significant. There is no equivalent cliché or meaning for males to 'It's a good job for a girl.' In her book *Just Like A Girl*, Sue Sharpe (1976) devotes a chapter to this topic and indicates the constraints that apply for girls when they contemplate entering the workforce: 'Part of the legacy of women's role is that they should be involved less with themselves than with caring and looking after others, and the upbringing of girls makes them dependent for identity and self-esteem on their relationships with other people. This was illustrated by the comments from the Ealing girls on the jobs they expected to get. The jobs they chose reflected, of course, the jobs that were normally open to them; these, in turn, were usually extensions of their "feminine" role and exploited some supposedly feminine characteristic.' (p164).

Sharpe found, as I did, that almost half the girls thought office work was a nice job for a girl. 'The next most popular jobs were as teachers, nurses, shop assistants and bank clerks— which altogether accounted for about a quarter of the job choices. Following these were girls who wished to become receptionists, telephonists, air hostesses, hairdressers and children's nurses or nannies. The narrow range of careers so far selected took up over three-quarters of all choices.' (p161).

'All the chosen careers' says Sharpe, 'were safely in the realm of "women's work" (with the exception of the choices of doctor and barrister).' (p161). These findings are very similar to my own where the reply 'I'm going into an office/teaching/nursing' was the most common and was usually accompanied by 'because it's a good job for a girl.' Teaching and nursing were frequently mentioned in relation to family responsibilities — you can always go back after the children go to school.

Seven girls in my sample made the distinction between what they would *like* to do — and what they would *probably* do: four said they probably wouldn't get a job, and three that they would probably work in a factory.* Sue Sharpe states that 'Only two of the Ealing schoolgirls expected to work in a factory.'

In this area — as in the area of work after marriage — the girls seem to be *unrealistic*. As Sharpe says, the choices of the girls she interviewed 'bore no relation to the national distribution of women's work which places most girls and women (especially those from working class backgrounds) in factory work, clerical work, shop work and service work (catering, *etc.*).' (p161). To be realistic here would be to cast doubt on the romantic myth.

When it came to work after marriage most of the girls I spoke to indicated that they would probably undertake 'part-time' work, but generally 'not while the children were young'. Only two were prepared to admit the possibility that they could be the sole supporters of their families. While a number were from single parent families (and with one exception it was the mother who was the single parent) and were supported by their mothers, sadly, they frequently saw this as their mother's fault.

Student: I don't want to work after I have children. It's not fair to them.

Interviewer: Well, you might have to, you mightn't have any choice. What if you get deserted, or divorced? There are thousands and thousands of women who didn't plan on working and who are the bread-winners now ... don't you think it might be a good idea to plan for the possibility?

Student: Oh, I won't be getting a divorce. I wouldn't marry anyone who wanted a divorce. I wouldn't get caught (like my mum). Women who have young children shouldn't work.

*   *   *   *   *   *   *

* I suspect the number who entertained the possibility of unemployment would have increased dramatically since 1978.

Student: I might do some part-time work, to take me out of the house. It makes you more interesting. Husbands can like having an interesting wife.

Interviewer: But what if you have to work? What if your husband dies or you get a divorce, or even if you have to work just to make ends meet?

Student: I don't think about that. I just think about having a husband and children and it will all be fine. And when the children go to school, I'll get a part time job. It doesn't matter what it is.

* * * * * * *

Student: You mean, like me mum? Having to work to support us? I'll never be like that. It's a rotten life and I'll never have it. I'll make sure I do better.

Almost no other possibility except the fulfilment of the romantic dream is entertained, let alone planned for. Although many students had some evidence in their daily lives that the romantic dream *didn't* always come true (from mothers and sisters) they almost always questioned the woman rather than the romantic dream. Perhaps this is easier (it is certainly encouraged) for it seems that for many, if not most, of them, if there is no role of wife and mother in the idealised version in which it is presented in patriarchal society, there is nothing. Paid employment (or life without men) does not figure as a viable and desirable alternative — not even if combined with marriage and motherhood — in the minds of most young women. And paid employment in unskilled and low paid jobs is rarely viewed as a probability (because of necessity) and allowed for.

I am sure that one of the reasons the transparent myth of wedded bliss and maternal fulfilment is allowed to endure is because the knowledge that individual women possess is not pooled, is not made cumulative, encoded, and available for other women. Feminist material which tries to encode and articulate women's view of the world and women's experience of the world is 'outlawed' over and over again in the classroom, to the extent that many teachers are apprehensive about bringing in certain books; plain covers and work sheets, where the sources can be camouflaged, abound.

There have been three occasions when I have been 'discovered' teaching the underside, the uncharted areas, where I have introduced such 'objective' material as statistics on divorce and depression, on sexual inequalities in work, in pay and promotion, and once I was 'reprimanded' but twice I was abused. I was accused of trying to turn the girls into manhaters and of destroying family life, and there were numerous comments about my own inadequacies and my embittered state of mind (for I am a 'target', being neither wife nor mother).

The entire curriculum can revolve around men, the future of the world can revolve around men, and misogyny, while not openly advocated, is nonetheless perceived as reasonable and understandable. But women, who have genuine grievances against male dominance, do not even possess a word to denote our justifiable anger; if we try to talk about women in a patriarchal society we are 'perverting' the minds of the young, and may even be regarded as unsuitable teachers.

I can only deduce that in a male dominated society it is essential that women do not make links with other women, that they do not pool their experience and make deductions and generalise from it. I can only conclude that it is crucial that women persist in seeing their future as blank, apart from motherhood. I can, however, document some of the devices whereby these ends are achieved.

I have also asked boys what women can and cannot do, and what women do after thirty, and it is my contention that they are more adamant than the girls that women are nothing other than reproducers. 'After thirty?' asked one boy, 'I'd rather not think about it. They're all old bags by then, that's why men go to the pub.'

According to the boys, women cannot be astronauts (see Elizabeth Sarah, 1980), they cannot be anything from air pilots to bus drivers (even when you show them pictures of women in these jobs). They say women cannot be engineers, computer personnel, telephone mechanics, train drivers, managers, doctors, dentists or lawyers (even when they may have, or may have met, a female doctor, dentist or lawyer). What women *should not do* becomes transformed in the male student's mind to what women *cannot do*.

Women *can* be teachers, social workers, nurses, almost anything that involves caring for others and does not enjoy high status or high pay. In this respect the boys were very much like some of the teachers that Stanley interviewed who directed the 'caring' female into the traditional female occupations. But even where the boys did accept that 'women have to do something between school and marriage' and that particular something could be 'a good job for a girl', they would not allow that paid employment could be a valid, major preoccupation for girls, or that girls could be independent of boys; nor would they subscribe to the doctrine of equal pay — with very few exceptions.

'Girls only work till they get married' declared one boy, and 'I don't like girls who talk about jobs like they were boys' said another; and they were not reticent about telling girls what they thought. 'When a girl starts talking about a job, I think she's stupid' said another. 'What's she going to do about the kids? They forget about them, don't they? But girls can't do the same things as boys, because boys don't have kids.'

Male Student: I don't think there should be equal pay because a man has to support a family and girls don't.

Interviewer: Do you think men without families, bachelors, should get paid less then?

Male Student: What? No! I haven't thought about them. No, that's good luck to them. That's why blokes don't want to get married, you've got more to spend on yourself.

Interviewer: But what about women who have to support a family, there are hundreds of thousands of them, don't you think they should earn the same as a man who supports a family or as much as a bachelor who supports no one?

Male Student: (Talking over interviewer) No, they should get themselves a husband. That's the proper way. Men should earn more than girls because they've got more responsibilities. It's right as it is. Girls just have to get husbands. It's their fault if they don't.

The principles of patriarchy could not be stated much more explicitly!

Unfortunately, because patriarchy has defined a specific role for women and a specific role for men in the interest of male supremacy, it seems that there are only two alternatives: students are educated either for motherhood or for employment. And if women do not choose to put all their eggs into the one basket of motherhood and marriage, they must put them all into the other basket of employment. Either way, they lose.

But this division is not the only one (although it might well be the best one for men); one of the resolutions put forward at the Cambridge conference 'Sex Differentiation and Schooling' (January,

1980) was *that there be part-time work for all*. It would seem sensible to me that *all* members of our society should be able to combine paid employment with parenting if desired, and that this should be a reasonable task, and not a double shift as it currently is for so many women. No member of society should be educated on the assumption that they will not work, and no member of society educated on the assumption that there will not be a next generation requiring care. While men control education and society however, they are unlikely to implement such policies precisely because they increase the options available to women and reduce the power and primacy of men.

Rather than seeking ways to accommodate women in the workforce, the current trend, with increasing unemployment, is to get them out, and for the jobs presently *usurped* by women to be available to men. The next few years are likely to usher in a wave of slogans about women's proper place — at home — which are reminiscent of the post-war period.

Already the writing is on the wall and indicates some of the links between a male god and a male value system: if God had wanted women to work, he would not have made them mothers, asserts Patrick Jenkin (the Secretary for Social Services). And Adam Raphael, that most respectable and reputable journalist, writes in *The Observer* that the current tax system is disgraceful because it is 'heavily biased towards encouraging married women to seek paid work outside the home'. It might have been alright when women were needed, argues Raphael, as they were during the last war — but not now when there are so many men out of work. (7 December 1980; p12). The Director of the University of London Institute of Education, William Taylor (1978) has stated that there are qualified married women teachers who 'for one reason or another are not currently employed' but who would be 'willing to teach again if and when opportunity permits' and who act as 'the *regulator*' (my emphasis), who help 'to smooth the curve of institutional change and facilitate . . . the planning of teacher supply'. And at the moment the institutional change requires that women go back home. There is little evidence that many men in influential positions think that paid work is central to women; the whole philosophy is that they are dependent upon men.

While most people might expect that the incidence of social dissatisfaction and disturbance would rise with rising unemployment, it is likely that women will once more be blamed; if women were at home with their children, where they are supposed to be, such things would not happen. 'Maternal deprivation' theories will be revived as the scapegoat, before employment, unemployment, and pay, are more equitably distributed.

As less money is spent on social services, as more institutions which house and cater for the old, the invalid and the ill, are closed, we are informed that the inmates are more adequately catered for in 'the community'. Who is this magic community? It is unpaid women: women who are required to work, but for *no money,* and *no status,* in order that their material and psychological dependence on men can be maintained. And schools will subtly reinforce this role for women, will 'educate' them for these future 'nurturant' tasks.*

I could not advocate that employment and financial reward be the central concerns of life; that such a possibility even arises is a measure of how far the male view of the world is perceived as 'sensible'. But I can suggest that while women are systematically denied access to employment, and to money, men will continue to monopolise the power in our society.

Every teacher who assumes that women will be preoccupied by childcare, who cannot visualise women in paid employment or living satisfactorily without men, who does not recognise that women in general work harder and that they receive less money, plays an active role in perpetuating patriarchy. Teachers who do *not* make it their business to find and present the facts of women's lives to boys as well as girls in their classes, are engaging in political acts, practising indoctrination, and presenting only one side of the story.

Once women are presented with the facts, we are capable of making our own decisions about what to do. Once we understand that we are being denied access to certain knowledge, to certain training schemes, to certain jobs, to equal pay, to fair demands on our time, we can formulate our own policies. Once we appreciate that it is in men's interests to keep us dependent, to convince us that we need marriage, to foist their share of daily maintenance and childcare onto us, and that *it is not in our interest at all,* we will be in a position to postulate alternative plans. At the moment we have *no* choice because we are provided with little or no knowledge about women's experience.

When educationalists and teachers spend the *same* amount of time and care documenting and presenting women's version of experience

---

* I expect that over the next few years courses in community care will begin to appear in schools and will be perceived as a purposeful — but probably unpaid — activity, for women after the children have gone.

as they do for men, when the world is described and explained from the point of view of women as well as men, and when both versions coexist in educational institutions and are accorded equal validity, then the future for women will not be blank. Initially we might not be elated by this information, we may even be distressed, and we will be justifiably angry. But we will understand that dominance and subordination are neither inevitable nor immutable and we will work for change. It is because we will be concerned with the elimination of patriarchy when we appreciate the conditions of women's existence under patriarchy, that we are deprived of knowledge about women's existence.

In the last decade much has been made of the fact that women are channelled into some subjects and not others, and there have been many suggestions put forward which are designed to interest more women students in the traditionally male preserves (mathematics, science, technical subjects) and sometimes to interest more males in the traditional female areas. I subscribe to these suggestions. I think they are valid and crucial. But I do not think that the pattern of male dominance will necessarily be modified, even if and when women comprise half the scientists, mathematicians, engineers. After all, women may comprise half the class in co-educational institutions, but the male students still play the influential role in determining what happens in the classroom. Women comprise half the population but men still control society.

Whether women do mathematics or English, science or French, technical drawing or domestic science, is an issue in terms of individual choice; there is no reason for depriving women or men of the opportunity to pursue any interest on the basis of their genitalia. But currently, the *version* of mathematics, English, science, French, technical drawing or domestic science which is *taught*, is a *male* version, it has its origins in male experience, is circumscribed by male subjectivity, and perpetuates the repudiation of women and women's experience (see Spender, 1981, *Men's Studies Modified,* and particularly, Kathy Overfield's Chapter, 'Dirty Fingers, Grime and Slag Heaps: Purity and the Scientific Ethic').

While males remain in control, the criteria will simply shift. Two centuries ago, male control was preserved by denying women entry to education: once women entered, the criteria shifted so that it was a particular *form* of education that was considered the necessary qualification for positions of influence and control. Interestingly, in the last century it was a *classical* education that sorted the public office bearers and policy makers from the followers: it was argued that girls were not sufficiently good at languages to undertake such courses. Today, however, a technical education is assumed to be more discriminatory and girls have mysteriously become quite good at languages (now that they are no longer the criteria), but are not sufficiently good at technical subjects to be equally represented in educational or employment contexts. And if girls *do* become equally represented, it is my contention that the criteria will merely shift again — while males are in control and while that control goes unanalysed in education.

The only education currently available is *men's* education. Demanding equal access to that education will not of itself — even if realised — change the position of women and men. Women's history over the last few hundred years is the history of demanding equal access to the institutions defined and decreed by men, and women's problem remains the same. It is the problem which is not addressed in education: it is a subject that does not exist, because it does not exist for men. This is the locus of change if women's future is not to be blank.

9 Single-Sex Schools are Unreal

What has emerged consistently so far is that there can be no simple stratification of mixed-sex classrooms into teachers and students. Wherever males are present, males are 'in control', and they are even able to control teachers indirectly. The strategies of male students help to ensure that teachers devote more time and attention to them, view them more positively, and plan and present lessons that are in their interest (see also Elizabeth Sarah, 1980; Elizabeth Sarah, Marion Scott and Dale Spender, 1980; and Jenny Shaw, 1977). Male students also exert considerable control over female students by limiting the opportunities for female interaction, discounting female experience in terms of the curriculum, and denigrating the experience of female students. While the web of male influence extends and expands, however, female influence appears to be negligible in the presence of males, for female students stand in subordination *both* to teachers and to their male classmates, in most conventional classrooms.

That the males should dominate is not surprising: in any mixed-sex group in society it is usually males who are authoritative, who are in control and define the terms, and there is no reason why this should be less true of mixed-sex classrooms than any other mixed-sex context. If educationalists were to acknowledge this problem and tackle it, perhaps my criticisms would be modified. But they do not classify this as a problem, for it is not a problem for men. On the contrary, many male educationalists continue to deny its very existence and insist that equality of opportunity prevails even while one sex is so demonstrably dominant, and at the expense of the other.

Of course, it is undeniable that mixed-sex education *is* preparation for 'real life' (as is often asserted), for in real life it is men who dominate and control; but this is *not* equality of educational opportunity; it is indoctrination and practice in the art of dominance and subordination, and few educationalists are prepared to add this extra piece of information to their claims. Single-sex education, in contrast, is an *unreal* experience and form of organisation, precisely because it does not provide girls with a group to whom they are required to defer, nor boys with a group whom they can dominate. And boys, it seems, do not perform quite so well when they have no one to dominate, when they have no foil against which their performance is enhanced, when they have no negative reference group which allows them to be perceived as the 'better' students. That is one of the reasons why the men who control education have declared that co-education is the sensible arrangement, for it is better for boys.

Jenny Shaw (1977) has carefully studied the three volumes of R.R. Dale which were designed to promote co-education and she says that 'there is a rather telling sentence in volume three where he says, when comparing the academic success of girls and boys in single-sex and co-educational schools, that boys did better in co-educational schools but girls' performances fell off from single-sex to co-educational schools.' Dale found that boys did better and girls did worse, but there were no conscience qualms about recommending that co-education was desirable. The reduced success of girls was not seen as a problem. As Jenny Shaw says, 'he wishes to sweep this fact under the carpet so he urges that the question of comparative educational performance of pupils in co-educational schools never be raised again as an objection to co-educational schooling. He argues that the *social* advantages of co-educational schools are so considerable and so great that they outweigh the depressed academic performance of girls.' (Shaw, 1977; p52).

For males there are undoubtedly many social advantages in enhanced academic performance, there are many social advantages in being perceived as superior, but what are the *social* advantages for girls of reduced academic performance? Male subjectivity seems to leave a lot out, for R.R. Dale is explicitly stating that it is socially advantageous for girls to be subordinate. Nor has he modified his view. Jill Lavigueur (1980) quotes a more recent scientific and objective statement of his in which he sees the 'natural' aggression of men and submission of women making their presence felt in the co-educational classroom:

'Theorising' states Dale, 'one might see aggressiveness in the male leading to physical pursuits, physical crimes, the desire for dominance, creativity, and urge to exploration. In education it may play a part in male untidiness, carelessness, truancy, rebelliousness, failure to do homework — yet also the drive needed for success. The comparative submissiveness and shyness of the girl' he adds (and note *the male* is compared to *the girl*), 'may be a factor in her more retiring and less physically active life, less desire for dominance, less inclination to accept posts of high responsibility — and the desire to have as husband a "manly man" to whom she can look up. The less "aggressive" behaviour could be partly responsible, indirectly, for the greater neatness and conscientiousness of the schoolgirl's written work.' (Dale, 1975; p8).

In the social order, states Dale, 'maybe nature intended man to be the leader and woman to provide the stability' and therefore mixed-sex education is socially advantageous because this is precisely what it encourages.

R.R. Dale is the 'authority' on co-education and his pronouncements on the topic have been enormously influential. He has always known that women students do not perform as well in mixed-sex classrooms but that men students perform better. He *believes* that men are naturally dominant and women naturally subordinate, and that the enhanced performance of males in mixed-sex classrooms is therefore proper, and in accordance with nature. Like so many of his male predecessors he has found, and promoted, a system which will help to ensure male supremacy. He has done his best to make his beliefs about the inherent inferiority of women come true. And he is a respected educational theorist who has been accorded legitimation.

It is significant that the only critics of co-education are females. Co-education poses no problems for men, it is a convenient arrangement, it is considered progressive, and anyone who is critical is likely to be cast in the light of being reactionary or old-fashioned. As the claims for single-sex education grow, in the interests of girls, we can expect that there will be more abuse levelled at the claimants — in the interests of boys. .

If women were equally represented in policy making and administrative bodies, R.R. Dale's thesis would have encountered a very different reception, for what was no problem to him would have posed a major problem for women; what was the logical and sensible arrangement from his male perspective would have appeared as most illogical and nonsensical from a female perspective. But women do not have any control over their own education; men control the education of boys *and* girls and they exercise that control in the interests of boys. That is why there are mixed-sex classes, where boys can learn to dominate and girls to submit.

In single-sex classrooms girls do not have to defer to boys. The teachers' attention and concern must go to girls; it must be girls who are perceived as the more able students; to some extent the interests of the girls can be catered for (although this poses an enormous problem to which I will return later); if there have to be leaders they have to be girls (although this does not of course apply at the level of staffing). By removing the group which dominates and excludes the experience of women, single-sex schools can allow women to express and validate their own experience, to develop some autonomy, to build some confidence. Obviously, Mr R.R. Dale would not find such qualities in women socially advantageous: they could well challenge his assumption that women are inferior and submissive.

In single-sex schools, girls are protected from the daily messages supplied by boys that the girls are unworthy. That such a breathing space can be constructive and productive is the testimony of many women who have attended single-sex schools (see *Women and Education*, 'Girls' Schools Remembered', 1978; No 13).

But what happens to the boys in single-sex schools? Some teachers have commented on the consequences:

'It seems to me that the boys create an inferior or outside group and level the abuse at them that they would otherwise direct at the girls. The least 'manly' boys become the target and are used as substitute girls in a way.

In an all-boys school a group of 'not-real-boys' gets created. They are called the poofters and the cissies and are constantly likened to girls. The sexual hierarchy gets set up but some boys have to play the part that the girls would take in a mixed school. But of course they are still *all* boys and so the results of the pseudo-girls still stand as the results of boys.

I used to think that the abuse boys handed out to boys in single-sex schools was just awful. It was nearly always sexual . . . I don't want to repeat it . . . but now I'm teaching in a mixed school I can see that there's probably just as much sexual abuse but it's not as noticeable when it's directed at girls.

In an all-boys school females are an unknown quantity and they are often a topic, but they aren't a positive one. There's an awful lot of contempt for women. I wouldn't like to be a woman teacher in all-boys school.'

Understandably, I didn't like being a woman teacher in an all-boys school, and Anne Whitbread (1980) and many, many others didn't like it either. Sexual harassment is almost too polite a term to denote some of the assaults. But in a mixed-sex school, the female students as well as the female staff can be the targets for sexual harassment.

If the experience of boys is considered more important, more significant, more valuable than the experience of girls, then it is understandable that some teachers should be concerned when *some boys are treated like girls* in single-sex schools. It is understandable that teachers should be distressed that part of the class is treated in this 'despicable' manner, and that this has ramifications for the performance of their boy students. But when it is *girls* who are treated like girls, who are abused and sexually harassed, the problem is not perceived to be of the same magnitude.

That mixed-sex schools have been organised for the benefit of boys and in the interest of perpetuating male dominance is a claim that is currently being made in many countries. Birgit Brock-Utne (n.d.) has summarised many of the findings on mixed-sex education for Scandinavia and the United States and asserts that in mixed-sex schools girls and boys are constantly being taught the lesson of their relative importance and this helps to ensure that males continue to reign supreme. For example, in Sweden (the ostensible paradise of equality) Brock-Utne quotes a study on mathematics teaching which demonstrated that 'boys displayed noisy behaviour chiefly in order to get the help they needed from the teacher. They managed to get more help in class than the girls, too, who on the other hand had to take longer with their homework in order to keep up with the lessons.' (p11). Brock-Utne indicates that it is widely accepted in Sweden that the boys are able to influence the behaviour of the teachers to a much greater extent than the girls, and the boys know this and hence possess the evidence that they are more capable of influencing their environment than the girls.

By such means can the 'passivity' of the girls be imposed, by such means can girls learn they are without influence in a mixed-sex school, and it should not be seen as surprising if they cease trying to exert influence, and become successfully socialised. This is a lesson they might not learn in the artificial context of a single-sex school, where if any student is able to influence a teacher it must, of necessity, be a girl.

In terms of classroom interaction, single-sex schools do not usually convey the message to girls that they occupy second place (although the curriculum is quite another matter). Brock-Utne has commented on the widespread phenomenon in Scandinavian schools of the increased waiting time experienced by girls in mixed-sex classes and has said 'Girls are overlooked to a greater extent than boys when they put their hands up', and she adds 'this "making girls invisible" should be an interesting theme for further research.' (p12).

But will it become an issue for further research? How extensively do women have to document an educational problem that affects women before it becomes a concern of mainstream education? As early as 1898 when mixed-sex schooling was suggested in Britain, Alice Zimmern stated that although the education of girls had become accepted as a right, mixed-sex education could undermine that right by subordinating the interests of girls to those of boys 'under the pretence of equality.' (p243). Her expectations of the future have sadly been fulfilled:

'The attempts recently made . . . to economize by teaching boys and girls together, abolishing the headmistress and putting a headmaster over boys and girls alike . . . letting the girls do the best they can with it, is only a revival, under a new guise, of the old idea that girls are not entitled to the same consideration as boys.'

(Zimmern, 1898; p244).

That we thought we were discovering a new aspect of co-education, when we began to ask over the last decade who profits from mixed-sex classes, is another example of the extent to which we have been misled and denied knowledge about women, and about women's views on education. Even in 1937 M.G. Clarke stated that 'so called "co-education" is as a rule education for boys of which girls are permitted — or forced — to partake.' (Quoted in Delamont, 1980; p107).

For almost a century, then, women have been saying that it is boys who profit from co-education, that girls are simply obtaining access to male education which directly and indirectly teaches the inferiority of women. But R.R. Dale did not include this evidence in his 'authoritative' work.

Since the early seventies Florence Howe (1976) has been asking who profits from co-education in the USA: Jenny Shaw has been raising the issue in Britain since 1973, and more recently it has been taken up by many women educationalists (see Byrne, 1978; Deem, 1978; Delamont, 1980; Spender and Sarah, 1980) with the only major conference on sexism and schooling in Britain (January 1980) recommending that research be undertaken on this topic as a matter of urgency. It is an issue in Scandinavia, Australia, Canada and Germany, but it has not yet become a fundamental issue in mainstream education.

The question of mixed-sex versus single-sex schooling serves as a classic example of the way educational problems are derived from a male perspective. There are many reasons for suspecting that some of the men who were in authority *knew* that girls would be disadvantaged but chose to make this information 'invisible' because such arrangements were in the interests of boys. The extent of male control is also well illustrated by the fact that those who have ventured criticism of these arrangements have been labelled as 'reactionary' or plain 'wrong'.

But many of the justifications that were offered for mixed-sex education have been exposed as fraudulent. For example, it was argued that girls would derive advantages from mixed-sex education because they would have access to boys' subjects that were not usually available in all-girls schools. But instead of finding that more girls do physics or woodwork in mixed-sex schools, we find exactly the opposite, for 'pupils make more sex stereotyped choices in mixed-sex schools.' (Diana Leonard [Barker]; p21. See also DES, 1975, Education Survey 21). In an educational context it has consistently been argued that equality of educational opportunity exists when girls have access to boys' education; but this is an absurdity, for while males are in control the fact that their system is technically open to women is nothing more than cosmetic surgery.

Even the claim that men's education is technically available to women is fallacious for the 'DES survey of 1979 of 365 schools found that "in practice" 65% of the schools differentiated between pupils by sex in craft subjects' and that there were 'schools where physical science was timetabled against a "girl's subject" . . . such as cookery, to discourage girls from taking science.' (Delamont, 1980; p49).

If certain classes traditionally reserved for boys are, however, technically available to girls, it is *still* possible for girls to be discouraged from choosing such an option. It has already been pointed out that boys can exert pressure on girls, harassing them, declaring them to be unfeminine, asserting that maths, or science, or woodwork, for example, are not 'proper' subjects for girls and that girls cannot perform well at them anyway. But even if the girls take no notice of such boys (in itself a considerable achievement, for it must be remembered that we are not talking of two groups of equal power, status and confidence), then some teachers can help to make the girls feel so unwelcome that they are forced to withdraw. Sara Delamont (1980) provides a record of some of her observations in secondary schools:

'Melin Court (4.9.78.)
In the woodwork room the new pupils are being allocated places at the benches, in alphabetical order, with the boys first. When

Mr Beech found he had twenty three in the group it was girls left without bench places — about three girls left to work where someone was absent (i.e. changing seats every week/starting each lesson by trying to find a space).

Waverly (20.9.78.)
Technical Drawing — Mr Plumb
There are more pupils than bench spaces so Parween and a boy are on the side bench, and three girls are down the front.

Waverly (8.9.78.)
After break go to Technical Drawing with Mr Quill. He lines them up at back and side of the room, gives them seats in alphabetical order. Boys first — leaving spaces for absentees. There are twenty eight in the class list so five girls get left off proper desks and given slots on the side benches. Then they are told they can sit in absentees' seats.'
(Delamont, 1980; p49).

As Sara Delamont adds 'Anything more calculated to make girls feel uneasy in wood and metalwork or technical drawing than to fail to give them a permanent seat is hard to imagine!'
While these are examples of the way males are provided with blatant preferential treatment in areas which are more explicitly considered to be their domain, it should not be forgotten that the same preferential treatment for males is being provided — perhaps in a more subtle form — in the rest of the school as well, with males receiving more teacher time, and male experience being accorded more attention and significance. The school is reflecting the patterns of society with this preferential treatment for males, and it is precisely because girls' single-sex schools can provide an *unreal* or *artificial* environment, when they remove male demands, that they can afford greater opportunities for girls.
But, in the case of single-sex schools, there is a problem for boys — for they do not perform as well when they have no negative reference group. While males are in control, single-sex schools are unlikely to be viewed as any 'solution' no matter how extensively women document this 'different' problem.
So if single-sex schools are not a realistic possibility, what strategies can women use to to ameliorate some of the existing problems for girls? I think there are changes that can be made within the existing framework which can be very productive. Annie Cornbleet (1981) for example has shown what positive outcomes can emerge when girls

are encouraged to act as a group, with rights, in the face of male opposition. This means that the girls have to be convinced that they are valued (no mean feat in the face of all that contradictory evidence) so that their confidence and self-esteem are enhanced to the extent that they feel capable of demanding their rights. Irene Payne (1980) is another feminist teacher who has made provision for teaching the girls separately on occasion and who has made male dominance in the classroom the topic for discussion. After having kept records of who did the talking, who defined the terms, and who got abused, the girls very quickly discovered for themselves that they were being controlled by the boys, and they acted collectively, in the mixed-sex classroom, to combat male control. And they were very successful.

At Stamford County Secondary Modern in Ashton-under-Lyne, it was discovered that while the average scores of boys and girls in mathematics were roughly equal on entry, by the end of the first year 'the average test score of the boys is significantly higher. Even at this early stage, girls are less likely to ask or answer questions.' It was decided that something should be done (instead of lamenting the girls' inferior ability) and in the attempt to determine the cause of the girls' 'decline' some of the classes were organised as single-sex groups for mathematics. Says Stuart Smith, 'The October 1978 scores indicate that at the time of the initial set selection there was little to choose between the girls in either set. By February this year (1980) the average score of the girls in the mixed set had fallen well behind that of the boys in the same set. In other words, these girls were conforming to the typical pattern of the school. The girls in the single-sex set, however, achieved a far better average score than the girls in the mixed set and were only slightly below the average score achieved by the boys.' (*The Times Educational Supplement* 18 July 1980). Smith adds that the school is introducing single-sex science teaching as well.

He also states that in the single-sex maths classes the girls are much more lively than in the mixed-sex classes; 'the working atmosphere is generally better and a greater degree of co-operation has been observed between girl and girl, and girl and teacher.' Do we really need any more red-herring research projects to locate the inherent deficiencies in the mathematics and spatial ability of girls?

It is not impossible to provide for girls in mixed-sex schools, although in many cases where such provision is proposed, there will no doubt be protest on behalf of the boys. (I have been told that such provision is sexist, and if girls *did* receive equal opportunities in mixed-sex classrooms, perhaps this would be sexist: but it is precisely because girls are in a sexist situation where they do not get equal opportunity that such provision is necessary.) If the performance of boys declines when they are taught separately from girls, rather than seeing the boys' performance in mixed-sex classes as inflated, many (male) administrators are more likely to argue that single-sex provision is unjust — for boys. Despite the possible obstacles, however, I think the campaign should begin.

However, I would not want unequivocally to endorse single-sex education for girls. Not only have all-girls schools often been used for teaching a 'feminine' role, they have also often been centres where male standards have prevailed. In the first place, it is easier said than done in a patriarchal society to suggest that women's interests and experience should influence the curriculum; the absence of such documentation has already been noted. And if and where such curriculum material is available, single-sex schools may still subscribe to the belief that male experience is what counts: single-sex schools may still teach military history rather than try to reconstruct women's history, if only because men still control the examination apparatus.

However, whether they learn military history or read male authors (for there are only three female authors on the prescribed list of fifty-two authors for three A level examinations), they will not have to conform to being 'silly or silent' (Florence Howe, 1977); they will not be trained in 'selective stupidity' (Joan Roberts, 1976); they will not have to defer to boys, dress for boys, or demean themselves for boys, and they will not be the target in the classroom for male abuse, and 'jokes'. I would prefer to see women teaching women about women— at least some of the time — and women assuming control and responsibility for women's education, but I will settle for a few sessions in a single-sex group of girls, where the topic for discussion is male dominance. I know why it is a forbidden topic in a partriarchal society: the results can be very disruptive — for male control.

Part Five
Women's View

10 Diversity and Strength

Whenever we set out to describe and explain the world we should keep in mind that there is one frame of reference which has its origins in male experience of the world and which is familiar to all members of society, and another frame of reference which has its origins in female experience, which may be very different but which has not been encoded, systematised, elaborated and passed on from one generation to the next, with the result that it is not a frame of reference which is familiar or even always coherent. We can readily see how women have been defined by men, described and explained by men for centuries as 'inferior', as passive and invisible, as powerless and resourceless, but *women* have not always described and explained women in this way. Today women are beginning to document the centuries of resistance and protest of women (see, for example, Sheila Rowbotham), the power of women (see Elizabeth Janeway, 1981, *Powers of the Weak*) and we should constantly be aware that there are two sides to the image of women, and they may share few resemblances with each other.

There can be no doubt that in the terms defined by men and valued by men, women have very few resources. While men have controlled the organisation of society and the distribution of wealth, it seems that they have reserved for themselves a disproportionate share of the wealth and allocated themselves a disproportionate share of the work. As a group, women earn less than 10% of the world's salaries and own less than 1% of the world's wealth despite the fact that they frequently work harder and longer than men (UN statistics). The pattern for women in capitalist societies has become one in which more and more women are undertaking a 'double-shift', performing two jobs while men perform only one (and as Ann Oakley, 1974, has pointed out, even where women are engaged in only *one* job it often entails longer hours and more arduous work than is the case with the regulated forty-hour-week, and it is not compensated by a wage). Despite ideologies to the contrary, Hilda Scott (1978) has suggested that the situation in socialist countries is similar. UN statistics also indicate that women work harder and longer, and for less money, in many developing countries as well.

Given these bleak statistics it is not surprising that part of our appreciation of women's strength and resources should encompass understandings about poverty, hardship, endless work and powerlessness. But it is only one side of the story.

Another aspect of women's subordination is that because they possess fewer financial resources than men, their vulnerability can be converted into economic dependence upon men as they are obliged to seek support and protection from men. This is a source of divisiveness among women as they are required to align themselves with men, even to identify with male interests, instead of aligning themselves with women. Having less money and less time than men has no doubt been a factor which has worked against women organising together in ways that men have done, and the isolation of women from one another has probably played a role in permitting patriarchy to go unchallenged on many occasions.

The divisions between women have been structured and strengthened partly because of women's impoverishment. While men have more than their fair share of resources, and women need access to those resources (and women certainly do need access to the other 99% of the world's wealth if we and our children are to survive) then one of the most common and sanctioned ways of attaining access is to gain the support of a man and this can invariably lead to competition with other women. Letty Cottin Pogrebin (1972) has said that 'Men compete for rewards and achievements. We compete for men. Men vie for worldly approval and status. We vie for husbands. Men measure themselves against (their) standards of excellence. We measure ourselves against one another.' (p78).

This may not be how all women see themselves in relation to other women (and with feminism, alternative relations are available and are being taken up in increasing numbers) but it is a relationship between women that is socially appropriate and encouraged, and it is a relationship between women which is hardly threatening to male dominance.

If men are holding the purse-strings, then considerable restrictions operate for women, who must ensure the continued good will of men if they wish to be the recipients of continued support. This is how many women find themselves caught in the web of working very hard (but work which does not count in men's terms) to be attractive to men, to gain approval, confirmation, and economic support from men. It is interesting to speculate on what might happen if, tomorrow, women could be financially independent and free: I suspect that many existing heterosexual relationships would end, for it is economic necessity, not choice, which keeps many women in such relationships.

Adrienne Rich (1980) has commented on the compulsory nature of heterosexuality in our society, and it does seem that while there are many forms of oppression, sexism is the only form that requires the oppressed to live in an intimate relationship with the oppressor. As Sheila Rowbotham (1973) has pointed out, women 'are subdued at the very moment of intimacy' and 'such subjugation is thus very different from the relationship between worker and capitalist.' (pp34-35).

Workers may meet together at the workplace, different ethnic groups may develop their own support systems and identity, but where is the space for women, even for women who are workers or members of minority ethnic groups? The system which has been organised in our own society — and many others — facilitates divisions among women and increases their dependence on men.

In fundamental ways women share this common experience of economic and emotional dependence, they share a common reality in which there are social and 'sensible' reasons for seeking the support of a man, and competing with other women. But there are differences as well, if not least because men have not divided resources equally among themselves and so women have access to different sized purses of men. Some men have more money and power than others, which is one of the reasons that the division and competition among women can be fostered.

In financial — and, consequently, educational — terms these differences are manifested, although they are differences which are usually derived from men and the social arrangements decreed by men, and which can be modified by men, as many deserted or divorced women can testify. One cannot just take the hierarchical differences that exist among men and transfer them to the women with whom they live: fathers die, husbands and lovers leave, sons move away and when the men go, so too, frequently, do the resources.

Lee Comer has shown the inadequacies of using 'class' terms to describe and explain women, for they are terms which have their origin in male experience and are often meaningless when used in relation to female experience. How accurate is the term 'middle-class', she asks, when applied to women, 'if the husband of the said middle-class woman goes off with his secretary, leaving his wife to fight for maintenance for her children, while she, without qualifications or even with them, struggles to find part time work

which fits in with school hours, defaults on mortgage paymen\
evicted, and finally capitulates to outwork and social securit\
everyday story of middle-class womanhood, my mother's included)?'
(p168). Some of the differences that have been structured among
women have very fragile foundations.

Differences, however, there are, and they cannot be denied, nor
would women in the women's movement want to deny them. Instead
they are a basis for exploration and validation and they are placed in
the context of the common experience of women. Again, there are
two sides to the coin and when many men (and some women) assert,
as they often do, that feminism or the women's movement is
overwhelmingly middle class and white, and therefore is to be
discredited, one can ask whose interests it serves to deny the validity of
this organised female force.

The divisions and differences among women are a starting point
within a feminist framework: they are not the inevitable end. We can
accept the existence of these divisions and differences, and we can also
resist them. We can examine how they have been set up, the purpose
that they serve, and the role that they play in perpetuating
patriarchy. And we can also see that they are divisions and
differences which sometimes give way to the recognition of the
common, shared experience of women. All women are required to
survive in a man's world and on men's terms in our society: all women
are at risk when it comes to male violence against women.

Racism has also served to divide and isolate women, and this is an
area that all women need to examine more closely. Currently in
Britain there are few opportunities for exploring our commonality
and diversity, for racism is so pervasive that to all intents and
purposes women are segregated. While we have been divided in the
past by race, there is no reason that this should continue; but it means
that we must consciously and actively struggle to overcome division
and segregation.

Because we are caught in a web of inherited meanings of racism,
this is often a difficult issue for women to confront, and it is an area
where we can be wilfully misinterpreted. In her article on racism,
entitled 'Disloyal to Civilization: Feminism, Racism, Gynephobia',*
Adrienne Rich (1979) says that it is difficult to begin to speak
'because I write at a crossroads which is mixed with pain and anger

---

* 'Gynephobia: The age-old, cross-cultural male fear and hatred of women,
which women too inhale like poisonous fumes from the air we breathe daily'
(p289).

and because I do not want my words to lend themselves to distortion or appropriation, either by apologists for a shallow and trivial notion of feminism, or by exponents of a racial politics that denies the fundamental nature of sexual politics and gender oppression.' (p279). As she states, it has been all too easy for 'the cynical and manipulative charge of "racism"' to be used against white feminists to stop them organising and for black feminists to be deterred by accusations of "fragmenting" the black struggle or "castrating" the black man.' (p290).

Rich points out that women did not create racism and have a history of being 'disloyal' to this institutionalised practice, but at the same time, 'women have been impressed into its service' (p282) and in the USA the 'passive or active instrumentality of white women in the practice of inhumanity against black people is a fact of history.' (p284).

Racism cannot be denied or ignored: we have all been reared in a racist society as we have in a sexist society, we have all assumed the values of racism and sexism regardless of whether or not we acknowledge the existence of those values. And racism and sexism have both been used to isolate women and to prevent women from understanding and recognising the common experience of all women. In patriarchal terms we are still divided but in feminist terms the differences among women can be a resource, not a limitation.

Implicitly and explicitly racism currently flourishes in many educational institutions and the problems surrounding racism are complex and require consideration and consultation. For example, Sara Delamont (1980) discusses the attitudes of some ethnic groups towards co-education and states that 'There is considerable evidence that the various Muslim groups in Britain include many parents who do not approve of co-education bcause it contradicts their principles of separate spheres for males and females. After puberty the respectable female should not be in the company of unrelated males and so education becomes a problem.' (p105).

Patricia Jeffery (1976) has said of the parents in Bristol that 'Most want their daughters to be well educated. However they are worried about co-education ... (so) ... Rashid intends to circumvent this problem by returning to Pakistan with his two daughters: Ruxsana comments ... "we shall go back with the girls ... We wouldn't let the girls go through college here — we want them to train as doctors in Lahore."' (p104).

I do not know the 'instant' answers to some of these problems (although I agree with Sara Delamont that there is no good reason for

Muslims not to have their own schools, which may be sex-segregated, in the same way that there are Roman Catholic or Jewish schools for example). I do not know the 'right' answers to the problem of teachers being asked to support girl students against their parents over arranged marriages or participation in games. But I do know that it would be racist to argue that single-sex schools for Muslim girls are inappropriate or that 'arranged marriages' are, by virtue of being 'arranged', to be condemned. *White* experience is no more the sum total of human experience than is male experience and it contains many limitations: those who are against 'arranged' marriages would have difficulty arguing that *love* is more adequate or desirable as a basis for marriage. From the perspective of women the controversy should be centred on marriage itself, on the economic necessity of marriage for most women and on the dependence it fosters and the constraints that it exercises, rather than on whether it is 'arranged' by parents or by the media. To discuss the pros and cons of 'arranged' marriage versus 'romantic' marriage is to conduct a debate entirely within male terms and is in many ways to divide women and to prevent them from pooling their resources.

For women do have many resources which have not disappeared simply because men have not seen fit to notice, describe or value them. Men may have appropriated for themselves the concepts of *bonding* and have described women as isolated and competing individuals, they may even have devised social structures to make their image of women come true, but women have also resisted these structures and images and have a tradition — albeit a submerged one — of co-operation and support. This is a resource which women must begin to utilise.

In some ways, co-operation and competition as *values*, are abstractions and they require some substantiation. I cannot turn to a body of research to indicate the way in which women co-operate for while there are tomes on competition which display men as doing very well, and which suggest that women are deficient in this highly valued quality, few studies have ever been conducted on co-operation — where the male image might not be so readily enhanced.

Some of the work that has been undertaken on language however shows the co-operative nature of women and indicates some of the ways in which they help to maintain social relations. Elizabeth Aries (1976), for example, has shown that when a group of men are engaged in talking, part of the process becomes 'gaining the floor': she interprets this as a 'competition' in which the 'winner' is the one who speaks. The same pattern does not apply for women where in group discussion part of the process is seen as ensuring that 'everyone has a turn' and Aries sees this as a more co-operative form of behaviour.

Because I was fascinated with Aries' findings I decided to conduct a small experiment of my own. In a group of all-male students, and a group of all-female students, I approached one member of each group and asked them to take a tape recorder (preferably unostentatiously) into their next discussion, to tape the discussion, and to *refrain from talking* throughout the discussion.

After these discussions I talked to the members of the groups. I asked the males if there was anyone who had not spoken during the discussion. Seven of the ten said everyone had spoken, and three named a male who they believed had not spoken. But their reporting was one hundred per cent inaccurate for no one named the male who did not speak and a check with the tape recorder revealed that the three who were perceived as non-speakers had actually spoken. The males were not aware of who spoke and who did not.

This was not the case with the female group where not only did the eight women accurately state who had not spoken, but six of them, voluntarily, expressed some concern about this. 'I wondered if June wasn't feeling well, but I didn't want to press her' one woman said. 'I think she's worried about something' said another, and 'I hope she doesn't feel left out or anything.'

Of course, it is quite possible that I chose a male 'stooge' who was not an 'identity' in his group, and therefore his actions went unnoticed, and a female who was an 'identity' and whose actions were noticed. But in my terms, and from my experience, I had actually chosen two people who were customarily quiet in class, and whose behaviour would not be perceived as atypical.

The male who did not speak said that no overtures to speak were made to him by members of his group, whereas June stated that it was difficult to resist the 'invitations' to participate that were made to her. Two of them were verbal but she stated that even when 'open' questions were asked, women looked at her to see if she wanted to join in. Many of the 'invitations' were not picked up on the tape, because they were non-verbal.

So what does this indicate? On its own, not very much perhaps, but within the framework that women are developing, it is consistent with the ideas about women's co-operation and awareness. It is my contention that consciousness-raising groups, for example, were not self-consciously devised by women and adopted, but are merely an extension of the co-operative turn-taking talk that women normally engage in. Women did not think out an egalitarian and considerate arrangement and then try and implement it, rather they found themselves engaged in this form of talk and attempted to describe and analyse it.

Mercilee Jenkins and Cheris Kramarae (1981) have stated that we can learn a great deal from studying the ways in which women communicate with each other. They indicate that there is evidence which suggests that in many societies it is the communication networks among women which serve as the foundation for social interaction (p16). They go on to say that women's work may also be the foundation of white middle class society — where women are often considered to be the most alienated from each other. As Elizabeth Bott (1971) indicates in her survey of the literature on family and social networks, female friendship has not been adequately studied. If we consider who typically writes the letters to friends and relatives, signed 'love Joe and Martha', who keeps track of social engagements, makes the phone calls to arrange who's going to bring what to the party, remembers the birthdays and anniversaries for both sides of the family, researches the family tree and keeps in touch with the grown children, spends the most time talking to the kids at home, makes and preserves the family artifacts, we see that it is usually women who do all this work. Surely these are the means by which families and social groups are created and maintained through communication and care (pp16-17).

Because women have had so much practice at communication and care, from such a very early age, they are often very good at it. They can create and maintain the social fabric, finding means of conciliation when those who are less skilled can frequently only engage in confrontation. This is an enormous resource and one which women can draw upon.

We need to ask why it is that these fundamental and valuable skills which are the basis for any society (which is not intent on destroying itself or other societies) have for so long been invisible or, where visible, mocked. We need to ask why these skills are not basic skills in education. And we need to know that women have them, and can use them.

Women have had and do have the resources of each other despite the fact that such resources are frequently denied or distorted. Significantly, there were *stories* in my family of the way mothers had supported daughters in the face of immense opposition, how sisters had stood with sisters, and regardless of the dominant ideology, how mothers-in-law had proved to be a source of strength to daughters-in-law. It is significant that they were stories, related orally from one generation to the next, and not encoded or printed and part of the conventional tradition. For female friendships have passed 'unnoticed'; they are dangerous, even subversive in a patriarchal society.

So pervasive has been the exclusion of women's bonds from the male record, that Virginia Woolf (1974) finds herself startled when she confronts, in a novel written by a woman, the phrase 'Chloe liked Olivia'. '"Chloe liked Olivia," I read. And then it struck me how immense a change was there. Chloe liked Olivia for perhaps the first time in literature. Cleopatra did not like Octavia. And how completely different *Antony and Cleopatra* would have been had she done so.' (p81). Woolf goes on to speculate on what our past (and present and future) might have been if the relationships between women had ever been a focus. 'So much has been left out, unattempted' she says, for so often women are 'not only seen by the other sex, but seen only in relation to the other sex. And how small a part of a woman's life is that.' (p82).

There are differences among women but there are also many bonds. Many of the differences have been devised and exploited so that they help to keep women divided and dependent; many of the bonds have been denied or distorted for the same reason. If women are no longer to be dependent then the differences that lead to division need to be overcome. This does not mean that they have to be denied or even eradicated but that they have to be revalued and reconceptualised, so that they lead us to an understanding of our own diversity and strength. And if they are to be redefined they need educational support, and education needs to be modified.

In 1938 Virginia Woolf brought together the two issues of war and education under the heading of male control *(Three Guineas)*. She found she could not support the existing education system because it did not develop an abhorrence of war, it did not try to educate the young towards understandings of co-operation. Rather, it interpreted difference as a threat, and conquest as a solution — for through it difference could be suppressed. It was men's education as she saw it, and she counselled women to stay *outside* it.

Her analysis is no less applicable today where schools and other educational institutions can practise on a small scale what nations can practise on a large scale, where competition, not co-operation, is the order of the day, where winning rather than a fair share is most valued, where difference is seen as deficiency. It is still men's education, and the same weaknesses, limitations, and exploitations are still valued. Virginia Woolf argued that if this was the 'civilisation' that men had created, women should be 'disloyal'. Adrienne Rich (1979) has taken the same stand. Women want, need, deserve, and will achieve, something better. Already women are creating their alternatives.

11 Women's Studies: Woman-Made

The late 1960s witnessed the re-emergence of women's concern over women's condition.* Almost spontaneously, in numerous countries, women began to ask questions about women from the perspective of women, and began to appreciate that there were no encoded answers (Joan Roberts, 1976). Generally, little was known about women, but what was known appeared to have been encoded by men or according to the criteria stipulated by men. (Much of what women had encoded in the past had of course 'disappeared' and was still awaiting 'rediscovery'.)

In large numbers, women began to appreciate that they were engaged in a 'double-shift', (for example, as they juggled to fit paid and unpaid work into the limitations of a twenty-four hour day), and it was not just that many of us felt this was *unjust*, we also began to realise that the double-shift was *unmanageable*. We could not continue to be homemakers and be constantly 'available' to our families, to be model cleaners, shoppers and cooks and meet the advertising man's requirements, *and* have full time jobs. When faced with an impossible task, human beings do not have many choices, but among them are the options of 'giving in' or of 'blaming oneself' and women had been resorting to both these options rather than declaring the task to be impossible — and unjust.

But in the late 1960s (partly in response to Betty Friedan's book, *The Feminine Mystique,* which was first published in 1963 and published by Penguin in 1965) the questions started to be asked and women began to turn to the traditional disciplines — such as sociology, psychology, economics, history — as a source of understanding and enlightenment. We combed conventional knowledge searching for descriptions and explanations of our existence, but they were not to be found. *Our* problems had not been perceived as problems.

* There is more than one explanation for the re-emergence of the women's movement at this particular time but Maren Lockwood Carden (1974) provides an overview in her book.

What we did find was that our double-shift sometimes presented a problem to men. We found ourselves defined in terms of the difficulties we caused when we were not continually available to our families: we had been surveyed for our greater incidence of marital disturbance and breakdown, for the stress we introduced into our marriages by our paid work, and for the difficulties we created for our children. Or else we found we were a problem for employers — because we were not continually available to them — as we attempted singly to carry out the responsibilities of *both* parents, and to look after sick children, or to meet school teachers (during the working day); or even to do the shopping or go to the dentist ourselves.

We were there — across the disciplines — as we impinged on the consciousness of men, but we were not there in our own right. Nowhere was our existence delineated from our point of view: our work which was unpaid did not even qualify as a 'topic' for investigation in sociology, nor as a 'fact' in economics. We were invisible.

It was in the recognition that we simply did not exist within the disciplines that *women's studies* was born: once we had come to accept that we were not included in the knowledge made by men (or according to men's rules) which was about men, we also accepted that if we wanted knowledge about women, from the perspective of women's existence, we would have to make it ourselves.

Our understandings were not forged overnight. We had all been reared in the disciplinary framework, taught to remain within the boundaries of the disciplines we studied, initiated into the patterns of those disciplines, and we were all products of a patriarchal society. Initially some of us were hesitant to declare the disciplines a hoax, we were reluctant to assert that individually and collectively they were of little use in helping us to understand the condition of half of humanity. The first protests came from within disciplines but soon spread across them.

In psychology, Naomi Weisstein put forward her critique as early as 1968 (*Kinder, Küche, Kirche as Scientific Law: Psychology Constructs the Female*, New England Free Press, Boston). The authorities on women were men, states Weisstein (and mentions Bruno Bettelheim and Erik Erikson) and 'they not only assert that a woman is defined by her ability to attract men, but they see no alternative definitions. They think that the definition of a woman in terms of a man is the way it should be; and they back it up with psychosexual incantation and biological ritual curses. A woman has an identity if she is attractive enough to obtain a man, and thus a home; for this will allow her to set about her life's task of "Joyful altruism and nurturance". A woman's *true* nature is that of a happy servant' (Weisstein, 1971; pp133-134), according to the men who are waited upon.

'Psychology has nothing to say about what women are really like' states Weisstein, 'what they need and what they want, essentially because psychology doesn't know.' (p135). Women have not made a contribution — as women — to the accumulated knowledge. But this has not prevented psychologists from pontificating at the expense of women.

Looking at women through the prism of women's experience, Jessie Bernard (1972) was able to document how marriage made women sick, but Phyllis Chesler (1974) was also able to show that psychologists made women sick — by the very simple process of defining them as sick. Because psychologists and psychiatrists (and the medical profession in general) assumed that the normal, healthy human being was a male, any differences exhibited by women could be readily interpreted as a deviation from the norm, as 'sickness'. 'The ethic of mental health is masculine in our culture' states Chesler (1974; p65) which is not surprising given that 90% of psychiatrists who make the decisions about what is mentally healthy and what is not are male (p59). Chesler quotes a study by Dr Inge K. Broverman *et al.* (1970) in which psychiatrists were asked to indicate what they perceived to be (a) a healthy adult, (b) a healthy male adult and (c) a healthy female adult. Not surprisingly a healthy adult and a healthy male adult shared similar characteristics, but a healthy female, in contrast, closely resembled an unhealthy or 'sick' male.

The healthy male was aggressive, independent and forceful, characteristics valued by men, for men: any woman who exhibited these prized characteristics however was 'unhealthy'. And the unhealthy male was deficient in these qualities, whereas the woman who was less aggressive, less independent, forceful, adventurous, rational — a profile that men do not want nor value for themselves — was healthy! This is how men have created 'sick' women, for if women show the same qualities as men, they are 'sick' and if they show different qualities from men, they are still 'sick'. For women to be healthy they must 'adjust' to patterns of behaviour that are regarded as less desirable and constitute evidence of deficiency.

Of course psychology was of little value to women who wanted to understand and explain the existence of women. And women psychologists began to talk about the bankruptcy of psychology to sociologists and economists (and anthropologists and medical practitioners and biologists and historians) and across disciplines the verdict of women was the same. We are not included in these disciplines, and worse, men are using these disciplines against us to impose their interests upon us. The construction of the disciplines was recognised as a political act serving a political purpose: traditional knowledge, with its compartmentalisation into the traditional disciplines, has been used as a means of keeping women in our subordinate place.

With the acknowledgement that knowledge served political ends, male supremacy was under attack, but the defences were, and still are, quite strong. It was possible for many men to hide behind the barriers — which they had erected — which were called science, objectivity and truth. There was a barrage of weaponry that could be used against women — it had been amassed for centuries — and from their privileged and protected place many 'authorities' were able to declare (and at times to convince others) that women were being emotional and neurotic, that women were introducing 'politics' into the pure preserves of knowledge.

Ten years of women's studies, however, has helped to deplete the defences of male supremacy. Nearly every university and polytechnic and many schools in Britain now have some form of women's studies course, where women are making the knowledge about women and in the interests of women. And after ten years, it is now possible to describe and explain what it is that women have been doing.

Women's studies is multi-disciplinary or interdisciplinary in that it is not located within the boundaries of any existing, legitimated discipline. If there had ever been a discipline entitled 'Analysis of Male Dominance' or 'Subordination under Male Supremacy' then there would have been a broad general framework in which women could have asked and answered questions about our own existence. This is the dimension that is left out of all the traditional disciplines, and which allows them to be collectively called *Men's Studies,* for they are the branches of knowledge that have evolved as men have addressed, refined and developed the problems of men, from the perspective of men. Perhaps when women's studies is as old and established as men's studies is today, it too will have as many sub-branches, variously compartmentalised and named. But at the moment, women's studies is more like the single, unifying quest for knowledge — usually called philosophy — which existed before the various disciplines split off. In a sense, women's studies is *pre-disciplinary*.

This is one of the reasons, for example, that today the voices of

Aphra Behn and Mary Wollstonecraft speak to us so clearly, despite the fact that they lived hundreds of years ago. For while the modern disciplines have separated off from philosophy during that time, for women it is as if these developments had never happened. We have not 'progressed' but are repeatedly asking the same fundamental questions, within the same framework. In the intervening years, the founding fathers of the contemporary disciplines have all gone their male supremacist ways, and have developed a vast and complex knowledge which, at best, assumes the non-existence of women, but more frequently has been actively used against women, and has been instrumental in explaining and justifying our subordination.

Against the enormous, accumulated knowledge of men, stands the recently created women's studies, which takes up the issues where women left off one hundred, two hundred, three hundred and more years ago. The task which we face, of providing a viable woman-centred alternative, is a mammoth one, given the entrenchment of men's studies, but already the gains made have been spectacular; already the deficiencies of every discipline have been exposed (Spender, 1981) and the problem of male dominance has been made central.

But it is not only in terms of *content* that gains have been made: because of the way women's studies is being constructed as a 'discipline', the very nature of the construction of knowledge, as it has been undertaken within the patriarchal framework, is also being challenged.

This has not necessarily been conscious choice on the part of women. When we recognised in the late 1960s and early 1970s that the only way to produce authentic knowledge about women was to make it ourselves, few of us realised the significance of the steps we were taking. We agreed that women would be the authorities on women, and we began by sharing our own experience, by pooling our understandings and insights. It was because there were no existing experts, because we were often even unaware of the contributions of women who had preceded us, because we thought that we were 'starting from the beginning', that we sought and accepted the validity of the experience of *all* women. In the same way that men have behaved for centuries we began consulting each other, checking with each other for similarities, differences, verification and validation, and reaching consensus about the parameters and realities of women's existence under patriarchy. But unlike men, we had no received tradition in which to operate. There were no 'rules' that had to be followed, no experts to be deferred to, no pre-existing models to which we had to conform. There were no established authorities whose reputations were vested in a particular theory and who sought to initiate us in seeing things their way. In short, there was no hierarchy.

In the absence of experts, courses, books, models, theories, we were all on an equal footing. No one was more learned, no one had access to a privileged way of knowing; there could be no division into teachers and students for we were all engaged in the same process of trying to generate knowledge about women, and the venture was co-operative, not competitive. Unlike the traditional model of teaching and learning (not discouraged in the main in the discipline of education) where a body of knowledge was assumed, where teachers were typified as those who were familiar with it and who imparted it to dependent students, where by virtue of their expertise teachers ruled what was valid and what was not, we had to begin with the premise that we were all equal, and that the knowledge of all women about their existence as women was valid. There could be no division into teachers and students in the conventional sense, and so there could be no privileged or authoritative group who could rule that the knowledge of some women was valid while that of other women was not. There could be no 'right' answers, and we had to learn to live with our own diversity. Our theories, our descriptions and explanations had to be able to take into account the range of experience of *all* women.

We had to learn to live with ambiguity and contradictions, to accept that there was no one, right, 'objective' answer, but many explanations for many phenomena. Sensitive as we were to the issue of exclusion and invisibility, we could not make the same mistakes as men had done, assume a 'norm' and penalise those who did not conform. We could not run the risk of leaving out some women, of denying their experience on grounds such as resources, ethnicity, age, or sexual preference. If we were to have descriptions and explanations about the existence of women, then *all* women should be included in the frame of reference, *all* women had to have a voice and be accommodated.

For many of us who had been reared with patriarchal models, this new frame of reference made many demands. It was not monolithic, it was not neat and orderly, it could not be tested by traditional means nor substantiated by traditional methods. We could not make decrees and pronouncements, we could not present the 'facts', for our understandings would not permit us to make such absolute rulings. We had become wary of decrees and pronouncements and disillusioned by 'facts' that were only 'half-truths'. We wanted 'better' knowledge, knowledge that was more accurate and more credible, and which could account for *human* experience, and not just a *segment* of it.

Already within women's studies we have begun to learn to value diversity, rather than to rank it. When the experience of all women is accepted as valid, then differences cannot be used to gauge deficiency or inadequacy. In the process of constructing women's studies we have, perhaps at times unintentionally, undermined the hierarchical foundations of education and helped to build a new educational model which does not depend on the 'expertise' of a few, and the unquestioned allegiance of the many. By our own actions we have begun to dismantle many of the supports upon which male dominance rests.

By demonstrating that all those who are involved in women's studies can *make* knowledge and are not passive dependents waiting to *receive* it, we have challenged some of the foundation stones of education and of male supremacy. Most of us are committed to continue.

Education, of course, as a discipline, (although by no means alone) continues to resist our efforts, to deny our achievements, and to discredit our ways of operating, partly because they are not the ways of men, sanctioned by men, but partly because they are subversive of educational theory and practice as a whole. If human beings can *make* their own knowledge then what role do educationalists have to play? (If women can produce our own meanings how can we be kept dependent on men, and the knowledge they have constructed?)

Ideally, women's studies is woman-made in a co-operative context: I say ideally, because in practice many concessions have been required in male-dominated educational institutions, where women's studies has been established. Within women's studies the concept of leader has been challenged, and as Joan Cassell (1977) argues, while there are admittedly 'leaders' there is consensus that such leaders should use their power and influence to ensure that *all* members of the group can become 'leaders' and this is a very different concept from the customary connotation: if all can be leaders there can be no permanently defined group of followers, there can be no static structure of subordination. The order of patriarchy begins to crumble. But our education system is still concerned with exercising a discriminatory role, in sorting the leaders from the followers, the dominants from the subordinates, the 'haves' from the 'have-nots', and our education system still sets the terms in which many women's studies courses are allowed to function. Compromises have been made over the last ten years, and the responsibility for them must remain with those of us who have made them; we are probably better served by having confidence in these judgements than by being critical. If women are to gain access to those circles in which policies are made we need to be on the 'inside' as well as working outside.

It is only within the framework of women's studies which is woman-made and woman-centred that we will be able to forge our alternative meanings and reconstruct our alternative past.* And these exercises are crucial for us, for through them we will be able to identify and analyse our subordination and promote change. Women's studies is women's education, and unless we are to repeat the patterns of the past, to be submerged in the immediate future and to re-emerge in the twenty-first century when once more women will have to engage in the work we are engaged in today, and which our foremothers engaged in periodically yesterday, then women's studies must continue. It is the means by which male control over education, through male control over knowledge, will be broken. And I believe that while men retain that control, women will remain subordinate.

This is not to suggest that all goes well with women's studies. It is located within an overall framework of male dominance; our descriptions and explanations are still often rooted in patriarchal understandings for we cannot produce a whole new set of cultural meanings in ten years (when men have had hundreds of years to produce theirs) and we cannot all instantly be resocialised and produce a new, ready-made reality. Besides, we *do* constitute a threat to the established order, and we should expect that manoeuvres will be made to control and contain us — and not necessarily by dismissing us, but possibly by absorbing us. Women's studies could cease to be woman-made and woman-centred, it could come under male control and become another academic subject in the same mould as the other conventional subjects. It could then serve male interests admirably because we could be told that women are especially catered for, that we do have our own little specialised area, a footnote to the male record. And we would be back with the descendants of Aphra Behn who were allowed to learn Latin and Greek, and the descendants of Mary Wollstonecraft who were finally permitted equal access to men's education: we would have gained little.

* This is not to assume for one minute that the only place where this can be done is within institutions: on the contrary we need the constant impetus provided by groups of women *outside* institutions.

Women's studies is not merely a matter of adding some women to the male records. It is not inserting a few 'great women' into the male history of 'great men'. It is questioning the very nature of history, it is asking why only the 'great' have been worthy of study, and by what criteria they were considered great. It is about investigating the experience of those who have been dominated and not just those who have done the dominating. Central to women's studies theory and practice (which, as Florence Howe, 1977, has argued, is a false distinction because they are often one and the same thing) is the issue of dominance, and studies which do not make this a central concern would have difficulty in justifying themselves as *women's* studies, for it is the central — and unifying — facet of women's lives in a patriarchal society.

If 'great women' are inserted into the history books, women writers studied in the literary courses, women's jobs included in the sociology of work, women's customs encompassed in anthropology, and women's contributions in the sciences acknowledged, then I shall express my approval because it is indisputable that women should be present when they have made equivalent contributions to men. But I do not classify this as women's studies, and I will not think that we have won the battle for our human rights, if the effort is discontinued with the achievement of some 'positive' images of women in the curriculum. Women will simply have made some ground on men's terms, and will be no closer to realising our autonomy, to gaining (at least half of the) control over our own education. Only when women decree half the terms will women have their own education and be receiving equal opportunity. And in order to do this we must generate knowledge about the way men control education in their own interest; this is a very different exercise from adding women on to men's education. It will mean that men's education, as well as women's, will undergo radical change.

If men's meanings are to coexist with women's (and it seems to me that there is no other way that equality can be realised) then many of men's meanings will have to be modified. At a very fundamental level men will have to abandon the concept of objectivity which they have erected and appropriated for themselves, and accept the limitations of their own subjectivity; and immediately they are stripped of much of their assumed authority and supremacy, and are open to question in a way not previously known. If there are to be men's 'truths' which originate in men's subjectivity, and women's 'truths' which originate in women's subjectivity, then it is obvious that there must be more than one 'truth' and this will have to be acknowledged and taken into account. No one group will have a privileged way of knowing and interpreting the work, and no one group will be able to choose its privileged successors in its own image, be it sex, ethnicity or class.

Much of what is known, taught, and received today will no longer be useful, and could be harmful, or humorous — as is so much that was known, taught and received in the past. For women's studies, which are woman-made and woman-centred, by their very existence challenge men's studies and point not only to their limitations, but to their oppressiveness.

Half the battle has been won. Women's studies which address male dominance exist, and even thrive, although they still fall short of presenting an equally viable option, and of coexisting on equal terms with men's studies. That books such as this can be written (and published) is testimony to the strength of the movement, but this should not be construed as 'success'. If tomorrow the 'demand' for books on men's studies were to decline it would be called a recession — but if the demand in women's studies were to decline it would be called a return to normal — the current 'fashion' would have passed. Many 'expect' such an eventuality and are in a position to help make their expectations come true.

12 Women's Education

In contrast to the museums, the libraries, the universities and other 'places of learning' where the accumulated knowledge of men is housed, are the few, small and underfinanced centres where women's knowledge — which could serve as a starting point for women's education — is maintained. The buildings which house women's knowledge are not at all grand or impressive. For example, there is the Fawcett Library, tucked away in the corner of the basement of a part of the City of London Polytechnic (and fortunate it is to be there too, for the collection went 'unhoused' for many years and was in great danger of 'disappearing' as it lay scattered in many boxes in numerous basements). There are other centres located in equally modest and inexpensive premises — such as the Women's Research and Resources Centre, above Sisterwrite Bookshop. They stand as a mark of women's lack of financial resources and women's marginality, but they are also testimony to women's resistance and resourcefulness.

Lack of finance and marginality are characteristic of women's education. In 1928 when Virginia Woolf visited Newnham and Girton Colleges in Cambridge, she spoke of the 'reprehensible poverty of our sex' (see *A Room of One's Own,* 1974; p22), when she contrasted the women's colleges with those of the men. She commented on the grandeur of the men's colleges, awed by all those 'masons who had been all those years on the roof of the chapel' and by all 'the kings and queens and nobles' who had brought sacks of gold and silver on their shoulders. Even 'the great financial magnates of our own time came and laid cheques and bonds,' she states, so that these great monuments could rise and grow. But what about the women's college, she asks? 'What lies beneath its gallant red brick and the wild unkempt grasses of the garden? What force lies behind that plain china ... the custard and the prunes?' (p21).

We can ask the same questions today when we see the way that the institutions and knowledge of men are funded, and the way that women's organisations and agencies struggle on the poverty line, never released from the worry and tension which accompany the ever-present question — will we survive? Dependent in large measure on voluntary workers, unable to pay high wages, frequently involved in 'exchanging' information with each other (as distinct from 'selling' it and gaining income) many of the centres concerned with women's education are caught in a 'poverty trap'. For example, at the moment, the Women's Research and Resources Centre must use many of the precious working hours that are available to solicit money from funding agencies and to devise fund-raising schemes. And it is perfectly clear that while such centres spend their time on these activities they are not producing and distributing information on women — except in so far as they are documenting our financial fragility.

Men have the money and they have used part of it to found, fund and foster their own knowledge about themselves, in which they appear in a favourable light. Women too need money — not for its own sake, or for the sake of erecting monuments and intimidating halls of learning — but to be free of constant worry, to be free to devote themselves to the task of generating and promoting knowledge about women. Thinking of what 'might have been', Virginia Woolf said, somewhat ruefully, that 'if only our mothers and their mothers before them had learnt the great art of making money, like their fathers and their grandfathers before them, to found fellowships and lectureships and prizes and scholarships appropriated to the use of their own sex' things would be very different. (p23). Woolf also acknowledges that many of us would not be here today if our mothers and grandmothers had been exclusively concerned with money-making. She also acknowledges that if they had, we still might not have reaped any 'rewards'.

There is another difficulty for in the case of our foremothers earning money was impossible for them and even 'had it been possible, the law denied them the right to possess what money they earned. It is only in the last forty eight years,' she said, that women have been allowed a penny of their own, and in comparison to men this is very little time in which to accumulate wealth. 'For all the centuries before that it would have been her husband's property' and this could well have discouraged women from trying to earn money at all. 'Every penny I earn, they may have said, will be taken from me and disposed of according to my husband's wisdom — perhaps to found a scholarship or to endow a fellowship in Balliol or Kings, so that to earn money, even if I could earn money, is not a matter that interests me very greatly. I had better leave it to my husband.' (p24).

In *Three Guineas* (1938) Virginia Woolf continued her attack on men's education and continued to contrast the resources that have been available for men's education with those that have been available to women. She comments on the fact that historically so much money has been invested in the education of boys, and so little in the education of girls; indeed, from the past to the present many girls have been required to make 'sacrifices' in the interests of their brothers' education. Today it is still not unusual to find many who would argue that education is more important for a boy, and that given limited resources, the money is better spent on the boy. This argument even prevails with local education authorities who, as Eileen Byrne has pointed out, allocate more resources to boys' education than to girls.

Even those who may wish to use the spurious argument that women have made no demands for education of their own, could be very quickly 'corrected'. For centuries women have been trying to organise a place of their own where they could explore and explain their own conditions of existence. In 1694 Mary Astell (of whom very little is known, of course) sought the establishment of a women's college; says Virginia Woolf, 'this obstinate and perhaps irreligious desire was alive in her; she actually proposed to establish a college for women. What is almost as remarkable, the Princess Ann was ready to give her £10,000 — a very considerable sum then, and indeed, now, for any woman to have at her disposal — towards the expenses. And then — we meet with a fact which is of extreme interest, both historically and psychologically; the Church intervened ... the money went elsewhere: the college was never founded.' (*Three Guineas*, 1977; p47).

If women did have money and did use it for educational purposes, then, as Woolf points out, they did so for men. There was 'the Countess of Pembroke who founded Pembroke; the Countess of Clare who founded Clare; Margaret of Anjou who founded Queens'; the Countess of Richmond and Derby who founded St John's and Christ's.' (p51). But who founded the women's colleges? What benefactors endowed them?

By the time the women's colleges came along it seems there was little left in the coffers. Such a small sum was needed and so little was forthcoming. We see the pattern of 'volunteers', of fund-raising activities, of the collection from small, private purses. We see the struggle for survival for women's places of their own – and today, again sometimes through 'economic necessity', we see some of these very same women's colleges, 'going co-educational'. There are many reasons for us to be distressed and disturbed.

All through the nineteenth century there were countless women who saw the desirability and the necessity of women controlling their own education, from schools to colleges. In the face of many and varied obstacles, from lack of money to open hostility and obstruction, women fought the battle to try and establish centres of women's education that were free from male control. If we survey the scene today we would have to admit that, one hundred years later, the dreams of those women have not been realised. Indeed, we might be forced to acknowledge that despite the increased number of women who have entered men's education, the position with regard to women controlling their own education is worse, not better. It is certainly not an area which is financially secure.

The knowledge which comes from the different experience of half the members of our society is knowledge which is produced on a budget which most educationalists would deem 'impossible'; it does say something about the 'cost effectiveness' of the male dominated enterprise, but it also says something about the initiative and energy of women who have produced so much on so little.

There is an enormous need and demand for this knowledge about women; but traditional educational institutions appear to be reluctant to provide the space in which it can be developed with the result that much of it is being generated in groups outside the traditional framework.

Within ILEA for example there are many, many teachers who are desperate for curriculum materials about women but their needs go unmet, even unnoticed, by the *Learning Materials Service* (with its £2 million budget). Numerous women have started to form their own groups to develop curriculum materials (such as the North London Women in Education Group) but again, they labour under enormous difficulties of money and time. So many of the agencies which are supposed to support teachers in schools go on supporting male interests; and women, again, are often engaged in doing two jobs (making *and* teaching the materials) while men do only one.

At the Women's Research and Resources Centre, so numerous were the requests from schoolgirls for information on women's history, it was agreed that it would be cheaper to produce a booklet and to provide it free, than it was to take all those many, many hours to answer the enormous number of queries individually. So *Women with a Past: A brief account of some aspects of women's history in Britain in the 19th and 20th centuries* (by Annmarie Turnbull, Anna Davin and Patricia de Wolfe) was produced, complete with cartoons. One little booklet (price seventy pence to those who aren't schoolgirls) to stand alongside, as the cover indicates, 'A thousand things that men have done: History from Caesar to Churchill.' A booklet produced after the demands of paid work have been met and before the demands of life maintenance are met, produced on a shoestring budget with all the extra details that such work entails (like trying to find the cheapest printer).

It is not only the schoolgirls who make requests: the Women's Research and Resources Centre is at times inundated with queries, to the extent that it has had to address the difficult question of whether to continue to meet these needs (and neglect other activities such as organising talks and seminars, monitoring current research, co-ordinating information — all of which are equally needed) or to accept that the task is becoming impossible because of its magnitude.

Among the queries received are those from teachers who want to know more about women's studies, who want to introduce courses on women but who need information on where and how to begin. They have turned to the WRRC because there seems to be nowhere else to go. In the entire (male controlled) education system of the UK there is nowhere for teachers to explore the possibilities of teaching about women: there are no teacher training courses in this area.

What women are organising for themselves in London is characteristic of developments in many other areas. Partly in response to the needs of practising teachers (at all levels) WEdG (Women's Education Group) has been established to co-ordinate and undertake research (as well as to act as a pressure group) and it holds regular fortnightly seminars which are almost embarrassingly well attended. The *Feminist Education Group* has been conducting courses on women's education for the last few years and, again, they are frequently oversubscribed despite the fact that they are fee-paying (this group was also established precisely because their demands were not catered for within an institution). The *Feminist History Group* has been meeting every two weeks (during term time) since 1973, and still finds itself with more offers of papers for presentation than it has places to accommodate them.

And all this is going on outside male controlled institutions. But it is unfunded and frequently unacknowledged. It is another aspect of the invisibility of women. Despite all the activity and all the information it is possible for many educationalists to state now (and to assert in the future) that a demand for women's education does not exist, and even, that there is nothing happening in the area.

While male educationalists (and those who support them) refuse to acknowledge the existence of centres of women's education, such education fails to find a place in official records. The *Women and Education Newsletter* has been in existence since 1973 and covers many of the issues of women's education, but it is rarely quoted or cited within the mainstream. Likewise, many of the inventories or surveys which profess to indicate what research is being undertaken within education in Britain fail to mention the enormous amount of activity in women's education. Not only does this exclude us from present consideration but when future generations look to today's official records to find out what was happening, they could be forgiven for assuming that we and our projects never existed. Males are acting as gatekeepers and we are not gaining entry.

If the official records were to contain even some of the data that is stored at the WRRC there is no way that future generations could be led to believe that women were not struggling for, and developing, a place of their own. For example, the following are the entries under 'Education' in the Research Index at the WRRC:*

Education:
ACKER, Sandra — Women and career interests — aspirations and ambitions. The invisibility of women in educational research.

BEECHAM, Yvonne — Career and job expectations, transition from school to work for women, curriculum materials, particularly social sciences for schools.

BUTLER, Linda — The local education authorities, adult education service and second chance education for women.

CLARRICOATES, Katherine — Sex role stereotyping in primary schools; the theft of girls' creativity; women teachers.

COFFMAN, Sandra — The effects of WS courses on sex role stereotypes.

CORR, Helen M. — Women and Education in Scotland, the position of women teachers, the Scottish Teaching Profession, 1872 - 1914.

CRITCHLEY, Marie — 16-19 year olds and discretionary awards (and other policies); nursery provision.

* I have confined the list to activities in the United Kingdom and I have not included the addresses of those involved. These can be obtained by visiting the centre.

DALTON, Pen — Women and art — girls and art education.

DAVID, Miki — Women's education and social policy.

DAVIES, Lynn — Deviance and sex roles in the classroom.

DAVIES, Rose — Sex stereotyping in infants schools.

DEEM, Rosemary — Women and education, especially higher education: school and work.

DUELLI-KLEIN, Renate — The development of Women's Studies.

DYHOUSE, Carol — Social history of women's education — 19th and 20th centuries.

EPSTEIN, Mady — Women's studies courses, especially the role played by fiction.

EYNARD, Rosemary — Women and mathematics.

FULLER, Mary — Dimensions of gender in school — self image and identification.

HAMILTON, Sheila — Social and economic activities of women graduates of Scottish Universities, late 19th early 20th centuries.

ISAACSON, Zelda — Women and science and maths, educational philosophy.

KELLY, Alison — Girls and science — international study of sex differences; affirmative action programmes on girls and science.

KENRICK, Jane — IQ testing, its origins and implications for women.

LANE, C. — Effectiveness of government retraining schemes for women re-entering the workforce.

LEVIN, Valerie — Women's employment and relationship to day care.

LITA-WSKI, Rosemary — Women members of the NUT.

LITTLEWOOD, Margaret — Married women teachers, especially recruitment in late 1960s.

LOVENDUSKI, Joni — Women in relation to political science teaching.

MATHEWS, Pauline — The women's movement, education and schooling since 1968 — curriculum development.

McCABE, Trisha — Doing feminist academic work.

McDONALD, Madeleine — Women and the reproduction of the class structure.

MILTON, Doreen — Part time teachers in further and higher education, and sex discrimination.

MOORE, Lindy — The education of women and girls in 19th century Scotland.

NAVA, Mica — Feminist influences on youth work and education, The Tufnell Park Girls' Project.

NEWCOMBE, Aliz — Women in art colleges.

ORAM, Alison — Women teachers 1910 — 1939.

PALUCH, Marta — Changing women's attitudes towards feminism, 6th form girls.

PARSONS, Gillian — Sociological perspectives on secondary English, implications for women.

RENDEL, Margherita — Women's education and women's studies.

REYNOLDS, Dorothy — Girls and mathematics.

SPENDER, Dale — Women's education, women's studies; the impact of WS courses on teacher trainees; patriarchal curriculum.

STANWORTH, Michelle — Gender and schooling.

STOCKDALE, Maureen — Mary Wollstonecraft and Education.

TAYLOR, June — Career development of female and male graduates.

TURNBULL, Annmarie — The ideology of home economics.

SAUNDERS, Leslie — Curriculum materials for girls and women, 3rd/4th year mixed ability.

SCOTT, Marian — Sexism and the curriculum, history of women's education.

STRUIGER, Maureen — Philosophical approach to the history of girls' education.

TURNER, Deborah — Women in teaching unions, 1910 — 1925, equal pay debates.

WATT, Alison — A feminist critique of health education.
WIDDOWSON, Frances — History of women teachers.
WOLPE, Ann Marie — Processes in sexist education,
     transition from school to work for girls.
WHYTE, Judith — Affirmative action programmes for girls
     in science.
WYNN, Barbara — Sexism and home economics, sexism
     and education.

   This is by no means all that is going on: some of the women engaged
in work on education are not registered here — for example Eileen
Byrne (1978, *Women and Education*), Sara Delamont (1980, *Sex Roles and
the School*), Glenys Lobban and Camilla Nightingale who have been
engaged in work on sexism in reading schemes and children's books. It
does however give some idea of the diversity of the work being
undertaken and it does indicate that there is a core of knowledge about
and for women's education, already in existence, and which is being
further developed.
   This evidence defies the oft-stated myth that women's education
— by and for women — is not an issue, not a topic; it defies the belief
that nothing is happening — or if it is, it is very peripheral and the
province of only a few eccentrics.
   But while we can point to great gains we should not lose sight of the
mammoth nature of the task that confronts us if we are to have equal
educational opportunities; nor should we fail to recognise the real
financial problems which thwart our efforts every step of the way.
   For centuries men have been encoding knowledge about men, they
have been developing what has gone before, they have invested vast
sums of money in the enterprise, recruited many researchers and
teachers, and have housed their words in secure and stately places. Our
current venture is less than ten years old and we cannot perform
miracles (particularly on our budgets) and produce the same quantity
of knowledge that men have produced. Nor do we want to. Quantity is
no guarantee of accuracy, as feminists have demonstrated; for
sometimes one feminist critique has been sufficient to bring into
disrepute whole areas of knowledge that have been developed by many
scholars over many generations (see Spender, 1981, *Men's Studies
Modified: the Impact of Feminism on the Academic Disciplines*).
   Trying to establish a coherent and comprehensive alternative to
what we already know, to establish the space in which to teach it and
the means to teach it with, is a task that consumes vast amounts of time
and requires extensive financial support. Some of the archivist work

necessary to find out about such women as Aphra Behn, for example, can spread over years and one book (or even three) on this woman is not enough to suit all purposes: we need biography, critical assessments of her extensive writing (think how many books there are on Ben Jonson or Milton or Dryden, for example), books on her that are suitable for schools, for further and adult education, so that the contribution she made is known to the many and not just the privileged few.

Think what a huge task it is to rewrite history with women as the central characters. It requires not just a different perspective or emphasis on what we already know, for women have been excluded so often from the records that we know little or nothing, and we must return to some of the original sources, seek documents and diaries that are locked away in old drawers which can tell us something about the way women have lived and what they felt and thought.

We cannot even undertake our task within the existing framework that men have set up, for our questions are different and our explanations cannot be accommodated within their schemata. For example, women are likely to ask questions about childbirth and are likely to trace the historical developments which took childbirth out of the hands of women and placed it in the hands of men (see Ann Oakley, 1976, *Wisewoman and Medicine Man: Changes in the Management of Childbirth*). And whereas the significant events for males may have been wars and revolutions, the significant event in the lives of many women may have been the introduction of birth control methods: for women accustomed to numerous and unchosen pregnancies the possibility of preventing pregnancy must have seemed revolutionary and most definitely *liberating*.

But this has not been the substance of history; on the contrary, liberation has been defined very differently by men and usually only as it relates to men (Lewis, 1981). For example there are two great 'liberating' events in modern European/American history — The French Revolution and the American War of Independence — and in *both* cases women — half the population — possessed fewer 'liberties' after these events than they did before. From women's point of view many of the great periods and events of history have been grossly misnamed, but it has taken many women much time even to discover these fundamental fallacies; how much more time and energy is needed to rectify them.

What is a history teacher to do when faced with many texts and materials (not to mention examination questions) that are concerned only with males? It simply isn't possible to prepare 'alternative' versions for every class. A concerted and co-operative enterprise is needed if women are to be able to present viable alternatives and to cover historical periods as they relate to the lives of women, and men.

The English teacher who seeks even a few alternative novels about girls and their experience of adolescence to combat the hundreds (thousands?) of novels about boys and their adolescence, may be doomed to disappointment. Elaine Showalter (1976) has outlined the dimensions that are added to life through literature which reflects and resonates one's own experience, but these dimensions are not made available to girls.

During my own teaching in secondary schools I spent much of my time talking quietly to girls about those physical and mental changes that confront *all* girls during adolescence and never was I able to recommend a novel that dealt with menstruation which could illuminate their own experience. On the contrary, the topic was taboo in many ways for boys as well as girls, for I know that many of the boys were also ignorant — and afraid — and would have welcomed an opportunity to explore this experience through the medium of literature.

Gloria Steinem (1978) has indicated that it would be very different 'If Men Could Menstruate'. 'Menstruation would become an enviable, boastworthy masculine event' she says. TV shows, newspapers and films would treat the subject seriously and at length, and sanitary supplies would of course be free. And what of the knowledge that would be produced if men were to menstruate? Why, says Steinem, 'male intellectuals would offer the most moral and logical arguments. How could a woman master any discipline that demanded a sense of time, space, mathematics or measurement, for instance, without that in-built gift for measuring the cycles of the moon and planets — and thus for measuring anything at all? In the rarefied (sic) fields of philosophy,and religion, could women compensate for missing the rhythm of the universe? Or for their lack of symbolic death-and-resurrection every month?' (p110).

Only women menstruate, and only men have produced knowledge, and men's relationship to menstruation is reflected in the knowledge we possess. The meanings of menstruation have been little explored or elaborated by women and yet such meanings are fundamental to our existence. We are beginning to encode them (see Weideger, 1978, *Female Cycles*), to make them the substance of women's education, but again one book, or one film, or one television programme or magazine article, is not enough. We need a whole array of materials, conveying information from a variety of angles, on this aspect of women's existence.

No one can state with any certainty what women's knowledge would be if it were to be fostered and funded in the same way as men's knowledge; no one could predict how women's education would be organised, although we can already see in the directions taken in some women's studies courses that what would be taught, and how it would be taught, could be dramatically different. We can begin to appreciate that many of the topics and issues which are today, within men's framework, accorded so much status, could become non-issues, in women's framework; and conversely, what may be perceived as non-data while men set the terms, could become crucial data if women were making decisions. What we do know, however, is that until the same opportunities are available to women to make knowledge about women (opportunities which have been available to men), there is no equality of educational opportunity for the two sexes.

Women's education does exist and is growing. It has many forms and many agencies and it is developing an alternative body of knowledge. When compared with what was available ten years ago, its achievements are little short of astonishing and are cause for optimism; but when compared with how much more is needed and the facilities available for development, there is cause for concern. At this moment the Feminist Archive, which collects material on the current women's movement and which is trying to write the women's record of the present, faces a financial crisis: the WRRC has held a series of emergency meetings to see how long, or even if, it can continue. Women may have few financial resources but even the few we have could and should be channelled into these autonomous activities of women. Supporting such ventures is an investment in our future. Men have many financial resources and it is time that some of them were channelled into women's education — but women's education that is woman-made.

Bibliography

ACKER, Sandra, 1980
"Feminist perspectives and the British sociology of education"
Paper presented at *British Sociological Association Annual
Conference*, Lancaster, April 8.

ARIES, Elizabeth, 1976
"Interaction patterns and themes of male, female, and mixed
groups" in *Small Group Behaviour*, 7, pp 7–18.

ASTELL, Mary, 1694
A Serious Proposal to the Ladies.

BARNES, Douglas, 1976
From Communication to Curriculum
Penguin, Harmondsworth, Middlesex.

BARNES, Douglas, James BRITTON, Harold ROSEN and the
L.A.T.E., 1976
Language, The Learner and the School
Penguin, Harmondsworth, Middlesex.

BEALE, Dorothea, 1869
*Reports Issued by the Schools Inquiry Commission on the
Education of Girls*
(reprinted with Extracts from the Evidence and a Preface, by
Dorothea Beale), London.

BERNARD, Jessie, 1972
The Future of Marriage
World Publishing, New York.

BLACKSTONE, Tessa, 1980
"Falling short of meritocracy"
The Times Higher Education Supplement, January 18, p 14.

BROCK-UTNE, Birgit, (n.d.)
Girls and the Hidden Curriculum of the Compulsory School
Mimeod Paper.

BRYANT, Margaret, 1979
*The Unexpected Revolution: A study in the history of education of
women and girls in the nineteenth century*
University of London Institute of Education, Studies in
Education 10.

BYRNE, Eileen, 1975
Inequality in educational-discriminal-resource-allocation in
schools *Education Review* 27:3: pp 179–191.

BYRNE, Eileen, 1978
Women and Education
Tavistock, London.

CARDEN, Maren Lockwood, 1974
The New Feminist Movement
Russell Sage Foundation, New York.

CASSELL, Joan, 1977
A group called women: sisterhood and symbolism in the feminist movement
David McKay, New York.

CHESLER, Phyllis, 1974
Women and Madness
Allen Lane, London.

CLARRICOATES, Katherine, 1978
'"Dinosaurs in the Classroom": A re-examination of some aspects of the "hidden" curriculum in primary schools' in *Women's Studies International Quarterly* Vol I, No 4, pp 353–364.

COMER, Lee, 1978
'The question of women and class' in *Women's Studies International Quarterly*, Vol I, No 2, pp 165–174.

CORNBLEET, Annie, 1981
'Schoolgirls — realities and possibilities'
Seminar, WEdG, London, February 17.

DALE, R.R., 1969
Mixed or Single Sex School?
Vol I — Pupil Teacher Relationships
Routledge & Kegan Paul, London.

DALE, R.R., 1971
Mixed or Single Sex School?
Vol II — Some Social Aspects
Routledge & Kegan Paul, London.

DALE, R.R., 1974
Mixed or Single Sex School?
Vol III — Attainment, Attitudes and Overview
Routledge and Kegan Paul, London.

DALE, R.R., 1975
'Education and Sex Roles' in *Educational Review*, Vol 27, No 3, June.

DALY, Mary 1973
  Beyond God the Father: Toward a philosophy of women's liberation
  The Women's Press, London.
DE BEAUVOIR, Simone, 1972
  The Second Sex
  Penguin, Harmondsworth, Middlesex.
DEEM, Rosemary, 1978
  Women and Schooling
  Routledge & Kegan Paul, London.
DELAMONT, Sara, 1980
  Sex Roles and the School
  Methuen, London.
DYHOUSE, Carol, 1976
  'Social Darwinistic Ideas and the development of women's education in England, 1800–1920' in *History of Education*, Vol V, No 1, pp 41–58.
DYHOUSE, Carol, 1977
  'Good wives and little mothers: social anxieties and the school girls' curriculum, 1890–1920'
  Oxford Review of Education, Vol IIì, No 1, pp 21–35.
DYHOUSE, Carol, 1978
  'Towards a "feminine" curriculum for English schoolgirls: the demands of ideology 1870–1963' in
  Women's Studies International Quarterly, Vol I, No 4, pp 297–311.

ELIOT, John, 1974
  'Sex Role Constraints on Freedom of Discussion: A neglected reality of the classroom' *The New Era*, reprinted 'Sex Roles and Silence in the Classroom'
  Spare Rib, 27.
ERNEST, John, 1976
  'Mathematics and Sex'
  American Mathematical Monthly Reprint.

FARLEY, Lin, 1978
  Sexual Shakedown: the sexual harassment of women in the job
  McGraw Hill, New York.
FENNEMA, Elizabeth, 1980
  'Success in Maths', paper presented at conference,
  Sex Differentiation in Schooling
  Churchill College, Cambridge, January 2–5.

FISHMAN, Pamela, 1977
'Interactional Shitwork' in
Heresies: A Feminist Publication on Arts and Politics, pp 99–101.
FRAZIER, Nancy and Myra SADKER, 1973
Sexism in School and Society
Harper and Row, New York.
FRIEDAN, Betty, 1963
The Feminine Mystique
Penguin, Harmondsworth, Middlesex

GLASTONBURY, Marion, 1978
'Holding the Pens' in
Inspiration and Drudgery: notes on literature and domestic labour in the nineteenth century
Women's Research and Resources Centre Publication, London, pp 27–46.
GOLDBERG, Philip, 1976
'Are women prejudiced against men?' in
Judith Stacey *et al.* (Eds), *And Jill Came Tumbling After*:
Sexism in American Education, Dell Publishing, New York, pp 37–42.
GOREAU, Angeline, 1980
Reconstructing Aphra: a social biography of Aphra Behn
The Dial Press, New York.
GOULIANOS, Joan (Ed), 1973
By a Woman Writt: Literature from Six Centuries By and About Women, New English Library, London.
GREER, Germaine, 1971
The Female Eunuch
McGibbon & Kee, London.
GREER, Germaine, 1979
The Obstacle Race
Secker & Warburg, London.

HALSEY, A.H., A.F. HEATH and J.M. RIDGE, 1980
Origins and destinations: family, class and education in modern Britain
Oxford University Press, Oxford.
HORNER, Matina, 1976
'Toward an understanding of achievement related conflict in Women' in Stacey *et al.* (Eds), *And Jill Came Tumbling After: Sexism in American Education*
Dell Publishing, New York, pp 43–63.

HOWE, Florence, 1976
'The education of women' in
Judith Stacey, *et al.* (Eds), *And Jill Came Tumbling After:
Sexism in American Education*, Dell Publishing, New York, pp
64–78.
HOWE, Florence, 1977
Seven Years Later: Women's Studies Programs in 1976
Report of the National Advisory Council on Women's
Educational Programs.
HUBBARD, Ruth, 1981
'The Emperor doesn't wear any clothes: the impact of feminism
on biology' in Dale Spender (Ed), *Men's Studies Modified: the
impact of feminism on the academic disciplines*, Pergamon Press,
Oxford, pp 213–236.
HUGHES, Mary, 1981
Private communication.

JANEWAY, Elizabeth, 1980
Powers of the Weak
Alfred Knopf, New York.
JEFFERY, Patricia, 1976
Migrants and Refugees
Cambridge University Press, Cambridge.
JENKINS, Mercilee and Cheris KRAMER, 1978
'Small group processes: Learning from women' in
Women's Studies International Quarterly, Vol I, No 1, pp
67–84.
JENKINS, Mercilee M. and Cheris KRAMARAE, 1981
'A thief in the house: women and language' in Dale Spender
(Ed), *Men's Studies Modified: the impact of feminism on the
academic disciplines*, Pergamon Press, Oxford.

KAMAROVSKY, Maria, 1946
'Cultural contradictions and sex roles' in *American Journal of
Sociology*, 52, no 3, November, pp 184–189 (as quoted in
Frazier and Sadker, 1973).
KEDDIE, Nell, 1975
'Classroom Knowledge' in Michael F.D. Young (Ed),
*Knowledge and Control: new directions for the sociology of
education*,
Collier Macmillan, London, pp 133–160.
KELLY, Alison (Ed), 1981
The Missing Half: girls and science education.
Manchester University Press, Manchester.

LAVIGUEUR, Jill, 1977
  'Equality of Educational Opportunity for girls: and its relation
  to co-education'
  Unpublished MA Dissertation, *University of Sheffield.*
LAVIGUEUR, Jill, 1980
  'Appendix: Coeducation and the tradition of separate needs' in
  Dale Spender and Elizabeth Sarah (Eds), *Learning to Lose:
  Sexism and Education*, The Women's Press, London, pp
  180–190.
LEGHORN, Lisa and Kathy PARKER, 1981
  Women's Worth
  Routledge & Kegan Paul, London
LEONARD (BARKER), Diana, 1977
  'Opportunities and choice in the curriculum', paper presented
  at conference, *Teaching Girls to be Women*, Essex, April.
LERNER, Gerda, 1977
  The Female Experience: an American Documentary
  Bobbs Merrill, Educational Publishing Indianapolis.
LEWIS, Jane, 1981
  'Women lost and found: the impact of feminism on history' in
  Dale Spender (Ed), *Men's Studies Modified: the impact of
  feminism on the academic disciplines*, Pergamon Press, Oxford.
LOBBAN, Glenys, 1977
  'Sexist bias in reading schemes' in M. Hoyles (Ed), *The Politics
  of Literacy*, Writers and Readers Publishing Cooperative,
  London.

MACAULAY, Catherine, 1790
  Letters on Education
MacKINNON, Catherine A., 1979
  *Sexual Harassment of Working Women: A Case of Sex
  Discrimination*,
  Yale University Press, New Haven, Conn.
McWILLIAMS-TULLBERG, Rita, 1975
  *Women of Cambridge: A men's university, though of a mixed
  type.*
  Victor Gollancz, London.
MEAD, Margaret, 1971
  Male and Female
  Penguin, Harmondsworth, Middlesex.
MILLER, Jean Baker, 1976
  Toward a New Psychology of Women
  Pelican, Penguin, Harmondsworth, Middlesex.

NEWSOM, J., 1948
The Education of Girls
Faber, London.
NIGHTINGALE, Camilla, 1977
'Boys will be boys but what will girls be' in M. Hoyles (Ed) *The Politics of Literacy*, Writers and Readers Publishing Co-operative, London, pp 95–98.

OAKLEY, Ann, 1972
Sex, Gender and Society
Temple Smith, London.
OAKLEY, Ann, 1974
The Sociology of Housework
Martin Robertson, London.
OAKLEY, Ann, 1976
'Wisewoman and Medicine Man: Changes in the Management of Childbirth' in Juliet Mitchell and Ann Oakley (Eds), *The Rights and Wrongs of Women*, Penguin, Middlesex, pp 17–58.
OVERFIELD, Kathy, 1981
'Dirty Fingers, Grime and Slag Heaps: Purity and the Scientific Ethic' in Dale Spender (Ed), *Men's Studies Modified: the impact of feminism on the academic disciplines*, Pergamon Press, Oxford, pp 237–247.

PARKER, Angele, 1973
'Sex differences in classroom intellectual argumentation' Unpublished MS Thesis, Pennsylvania State University.
PAYNE, Irene, 1980
'Materials for the classroom' in Dale Spender and Elizabeth Sarah (Eds), *Learning to Lose: Sexism and Education*, The Women's Press, London, pp 191–193.
POGREBIN, Letty Cottin, 1972
'Competing with Men'
MS I, No 2, p 78.

RAPHAEL, Adam, 1980
'Mother's place is in the home'
The Observer, December 7, p 12.
RICH, Adrienne, 1979
On Lies, Secrets and Silence
Virago, London.

RICH, Adrienne, 1980
'Compulsory Heterosexuality' in *Signs*, Vol 5, No 4, pp
631–660.
ROBERTS, Helen (Ed), 1981
Doing Feminist Research
Routledge & Kegan Paul, London.
ROBERTS, Joan (Ed), 1976
Beyond Intellectual Sexism: A new woman, a new reality
David McKay, New York.
ROSSI, Alice, 1970
John Stuart Mill and Harriet Taylor Mill: Essays on Sex Equality
University of Chicago Press.
ROWBOTHAM, Sheila, 1973
Woman's Consciousness, Man's World
Penguin, Harmondsworth, Middlesex.
ROWBOTHAM, Sheila, 1974
Women, Resistance and Revolution
Penguin, Harmondsworth, Middlesex.
ROWBOTHAM, Sheila, 1975
Hidden from History
Penguin, Harmondsworth, Middlesex.
RUTH, Sheila, 1980
Issues in Feminism: a first course in women's studies
Houghton Mifflin, Boston.

SCOTT, Hilda, 1978
'Eastern European Women in Theory and Practice' in
Women's Studies International Quarterly, Vol I, No 2, pp
189–200.
SCOTT, Marion, 1980
'Teach her a lesson: sexist curriculum in patriarchal education'
in Dale Spender and Elizabeth Sarah (Eds), *Learning to Lose:
Sexism and Education*, The Women's Press, London, pp
97–120.
SEARS, Pauline and David H. FELDMAN, 1976
'Teacher interaction with boys and girls' in Judith Stacey *et al.*
(Eds), *And Jill Came Tumbling After: Sexism in American
Education*, Dell Publishing, New York, pp 147–158.
SHARPE, Sue 1976
Just Like a Girl: how girls learn to be women
Penguin, Harmondsworth, Middlesex.

SHAW, Jenny, 1976
'Finishing schools: some implications of sex segregated education' in Diana Barker and Sheila Allen (Eds), *Sexual Divisions and Society: Process and Change*, Tavistock, London, pp 150–173.

SHAW, Jenny, 1977
'Sexual divisions in the classroom', paper presented at conference, *Teaching Girls to be Women*, Essex, April.

SHOWALTER, Elaine, 1976
"Women and the literary curriculum" in Stacey *et al.* (Eds) *And Jill Came Tumbling After: Sexism in American Education*. Dell Publishing, New York, pp 317–327.

SIMPSON, Hilary, 1979
'A literary trespasser: D.H. Lawrence's use of women's writing' in *Women's Studies International Quarterly*, Vol II, No. 2, pp 155–170.

SMITH, Dorothy, 1978
'A peculiar eclipsing: women's exclusion from man's culture' in *Women's Studies International Quarterly*, Vol I, No 4, pp 281–296.

SMITH, Stuart, 1980
'Should they be kept apart?'
Times Educational Supplement, July 18, p. 36.

'SOPHIA: A Person of Quality', 1739
Woman Not Inferior to Man: or, short and modest Vindication of the Natural Right of the Fair Sex to a perfect Equality of Power, Dignity and Esteem with the Men, John Hawkins, London Facsimile Reprint, 1975, Brentham Press, London.

SPENCER, Herbert, 1861
Education: Intellectual, Moral and Physical, London.

SPENCER, Herbert, 1876
Principles of Sociology, London.

SPENCER, Margaret and Moira G. McKENZIE, 1975
'Learning to read and the reading process' in Harold Rosen (Ed), *Language and Literacy in our Schools: some appraisals of the Bullock Report*.
Studies in Education 1, University of London Institute of Education, pp 7–27.

SPENDER, Dale, 1978
'The facts of life: sex differentiated knowledge in the English classroom and the school' in *English in Education*, Vol 12, No 3, Autumn, pp 1–9.

SPENDER, Dale, 1980
   Man Made Language
   Routledge & Kegan Paul, London.
SPENDER, Dale, 1980
   'Education or indoctrination?' in Dale Spender and Elizabeth
   Sarah (Eds), *Learning to Lose: Sexism and Education*, The
   Women's Press, London, pp 22–31.
SPENDER, Dale 1981 (a)
   'The role of teachers — what choices do they have?' paper
   prepared for Council for Cultural Co-operation, *Educational
   Research Workshop on Sex Stereotyping in Schools*, Norway,
   May 4–8.
SPENDER, Dale (Ed), 1981
   *Men's Studies Modified: the impact of feminism on the academic
   disciplines*, Pergamon Press, Oxford.
SPENDER, Dale, 1981 (b)
   'Education: the patriarchal paradigm and the response to
   feminism' in Dale Spender (Ed), *Men's Studies Modified: the
   impact of feminism on the academic disciplines*, Pergamon Press,
   Oxford, pp 155–173.
SPENDER, Lynne
   Unpublished Heritage: The Politics of Selection
   Routledge & Kegan Paul, London.
STANWORTH, Michelle, 1981
   *Gender and Schooling: A Study of Sexual Divisions in the
   Classroom*, Women's Research and Resources Centre
   Publication, London.
STEINEM, Gloria, 1978
   'If Men Could Menstruate'
   MS, October p 110.

TAYLOR, William, 1978
   Research and Reform in Teacher Education.
   Council of Europe/NFER Publishing Co.
TOBIAS, Sheila, 1978
   'Women's Studies: its origins, organisation and prospects'
   in *Women's Studies International Quarterly*, Vol I, No 1, pp
   85–98.
TOBIAS, Sheila, 1978 (b)
   Overcoming Math Anxiety
   Norton, New York.

TRUDGILL, Peter, 1975 (a)
Sociolinguistics: an introduction
Penguin, Harmondsworth, Middlesex.
TRUDGILL, Peter, 1975 (b)
'Sex, covert prestige and linguistic change in the urban British
English of Norwich' in Barrie Thorne and Nancy Henley (Eds),
Language and Sex; difference and dominance, Newbury House,
Massachusetts, pp 88–104.
TURNBULL, Annmarie, Anna DAVIN and Patricia de
WOLFE, 1980
*Women with a Past: a brief account of some aspects of women's
history in the 19th and 20th centuries.*
Women's Research and Resources Centre, London.

WALLEN, Paul, 1950
'Cultural contradictions and Sex roles: a repeat study' in
American Sociological Review, 15, no 2, March, pp 288–293.
WEIDEGER, Paula, 1978
Female Cycles
The Women's Press, London.
WEISSTEIN, Naomi, 1971
'Psychology constructs the female and the fantasy life of the
male psychologist' in Vivian Gornick and Barbara Moran
(Eds) *Woman in Sexist Society; studies in power and
powerlessness*, Basic Books, New York, pp 133–146.
WHITBREAD, Anne, 1980
'Female teachers are women first; sexual harassment at work'
in Dale Spender and Elizabeth Sarah (Eds), *Learning to Lose:
Sexism and Education*, The Women's Press, London, pp 90–96.
WOLLSTONECRAFT, Mary, 1978
A Vindication of the Rights of Woman
(First published 1792, J. Johnson, London.)
(Edited by Miriam Kramnick)
Pelican Classic, Penguin Books, Harmondsworth, Middlesex.
WOOLF, Virginia, 1933
Three Guineas
The Hogarth Press, London (reprinted 1977).
WOOLF, Virginia, 1974
A Room of One's Own
Penguin, Harmondsworth, Middlesex.

ZIMMERN, Alice, 1898
The Renaissance of Girls' Education in England
Innes, London.